Someone There for Me

Everyday Heroes
Through the
Eyes of Teens
in Foster Care

Edited by National Court Appointed Special Advocate Association

CWLA Press • Washington, DC

CWLA Press is an imprint of the Child Welfare League of America. The Child Welfare League of America is the nation's oldest and largest membership-based child welfare organization. We are committed to engaging people everywhere in promoting the well-being of children, youth, and their families, and protecting every child from harm.

CHILD WELFARE LEAGUE OF AMERICA, INC.
HEADQUARTERS
440 First Street, NW, Third Floor, Washington, DC 20001-2085
E-mail: books@cwla.org

CURRENT PRINTING (last digit)
10 9 8 7 6 5 4 3 2 1

Cover and text design by Jennifer R. Geanakos
Editing and introductions by Kristen L. K. Fletcher

Printed in the United States of America

ISBN # 1-58760-006-4

Library of Congress Cataloging-in-Publication Data
Someone there for me : everyday heroes through the eyes of teens in foster care.
   p. cm.
    ISBN 1-58760-006-4 (alk. paper)
     1. Volunteer workers in child welfare—United States—Case studies. 2. Foster children—United States--Case studies. 3. Social work with teenagers—United States--Case studies. I. Child Welfare League of America. II. National Court Appointed Special Advocates Organization. III. Title.

HV742.S65 2004
362.73'3'092273--dc22   2004003891

This book was produced in part through the generosity of the American Legion Child Welfare Foundation and the American Legion Auxiliary.

This project was supported by Cooperative Agreement No. 2002-CH-BX-K001 from the Office of Juvenile Justice and Delinquency Prevention, Office of Justice Programs, U.S. Department of Justice. Points of view or opinions in this document are those of the author and do not necessarily represent the official position or policies of the U.S. Department of Justice.

Contents

* **National CASA Essay Contest Grand Prize Winner**

Foreword

Someone Stood Up for Me

Antwone Fisher

In the summer of 1970, two things happened in our neighborhood in the Glenville area of Cleveland, Ohio, where I lived with my foster parents.

First, my foster mother's daughter and grandchildren came to stay with us for summer break. The grandchildren were my age, about 11 years old, and we got along very well. We were all fast friends and having a good time until the second thing happened.

A new family moved in next door. There was a mother, father and their four boys. We quickly learned that they were a family of bullies, headed by the father and sanctioned by the mother. It wasn't long before we were bickering over the fence, children and adults, and the bickering was about to escalate beyond words.

It was an "us against them" situation and I was ready to defend our side of the fence. Ready, that is, until my foster mother's daughter exclaimed to the neighbors, "Well, nobody better not put their hands on any of *my* children!"

With that comment, she drew a line between me and the other children, making it clear that I was excluded from her protection.

I needed her to speak up for me, too, and she let me down. It reminded me that I was unrepresented, I had no one who would defend me. I felt hollow and lonely. All these feelings were familiar to me, but on this day they hurt me even more.

A few years later, when my foster mother decided that she wanted out of the foster care business, she threw me out of her house into the pouring rain, telling me to go back where I came from.

I ended up in the lobby of the social services office where I met my caseworker, Patricia Nees. Miss Nees was not certain where to place me and she was taken aback by my sudden appearance there.

While Miss Nees and I spoke, my foster mother walked through the door, accusing me of robbing her. Her foolish pride brought her there. She could not bear the Department of Children and Family Services thinking that she was so callous as to toss me out in the rain.

Traveling all the way down to the social services office that morning, I had convinced myself that the years of abuse in that home were finally over, but there she stood.

How could I prove her accusations of robbery were untrue? I was desperate, so I began taking off my socks and shoes and turning my pockets inside out to show that I had nothing that belonged to my foster mother. I would have stripped myself naked right there in the lobby to prove her accusations false. But then Miss Nees told me to put my pockets back in, tuck in my shirt, and put my socks and shoes back on my feet.

Miss Nees turned to my foster mother and said with a steady gaze, "Unless there is something else you want to say, there's no need for you to stay." With those few simple words, my foster mother was neutralized. Her accusations became empty.

Even though I had nothing in this world to call my own, not even a voice, I felt victorious and powerful and protected because—for the first time in my life—someone spoke up for me. Someone defended me and it mattered. I felt secure. I had something more than just me. Miss Nees cared.

The children whose stories fill this book also had someone who stood up for them when it mattered most. Many had volunteer child advocates called CASA volunteers or volunteer guardians ad litem, and some had caring case workers like Miss Nees.

I can identify with their stories. It's not as if my 13 social workers didn't care for me, but most were young and probably just moving through the system before deciding whether social work would be a career for them.

I always thought they saw the world through rose-colored glasses. They saw that I was neat and clean, but quiet. They assumed I was well cared for, but shy. Unbeknownst to them, I was living in horror.

I could not relate to them. They seemed too distant from my reality. Still, I looked forward to my meetings with them. I thought that, if they asked me the right questions, I just might have the courage to tell someone what was actually happening in the foster home. It may be hard to imagine, but I didn't know to ask for help.

I needed someone like Tracey Walden, who worked with Elizabeth Velasquez to express her feelings openly. Reading her story, I remember feeling as if I had permission to say only what was asked of me. But Tracey gave Elizabeth power by making it okay to express her feelings with her own voice.

The act of self-expression builds inner strength and that can lead to a successful human being. It's a priceless gift to give a child. It's a gift that CASA volunteers are giving to children every day.

Pamela Butler tells the story of how a judge ruled that she should return to her birthmother—over Pamela's protests and those of Pat James, Pamela's CASA. The judge told Pamela, "You are young and you don't know what's best for you." But that judge didn't have to live with her mother.

The order was difficult for Pamela to accept, but at least she didn't have to stand in front of the judge and hear it alone. She had her CASA. Someone had stood up for her.

My children have my wife and me to speak for them, but some children are not as fortunate. CASA volunteers stand ready to give understanding, protection, care, and even love. When foster youth feel small and inconsequential, CASA volunteers articulate their feelings and thoughts to people who can help.

Pamela Butler writes, "To give a child a CASA is to give them a voice. To give them a voice is to give them hope, and to give them hope is to give them the world. I believe that with all my heart."

And me, I do, as well.

Essays

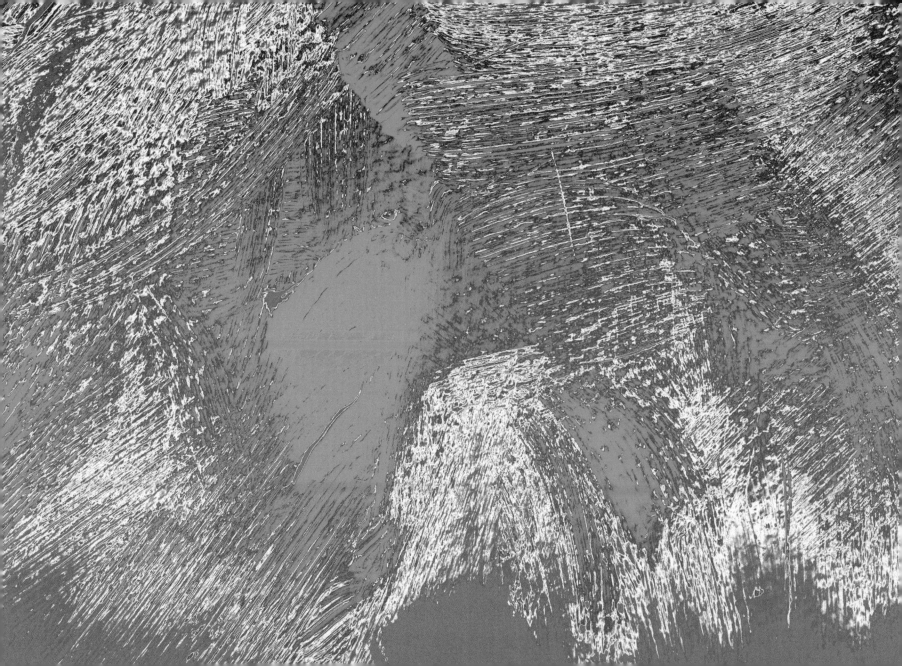

Pamela Butler
Salem, Oregon
CASA of Clackamas County

"We moved a lot and we weren't in school a lot," 19-year-old Pamela Butler, a former foster child, says of an early childhood spent moving from the family car to homeless shelters to motels. She says her mother would buy educational workbooks on sale at the drug store and, from them, taught her young daughter to read. Pamela relished those workbooks and the journals and notebooks she filled with her thoughts and poems. And although her life would continue to have more years of chaos than calm, Pamela clung to the possibilities in education and to the power of words.

Pat James, Pamela's CASA volunteer, believes Pamela decided long before she even got to high school that she would find her acceptance and success in academic pursuits. So she gave school everything, even entire nights spent studying. "School was her haven," says Pat. Her haven from a home she knew she would be better off away from and her one constant through a string of caseworkers, foster homes, attorneys, and bad experiences. Her one constant, along with Pat James.

Pat believed her job with Pamela was to bring some hope into bad situations and earn the trust of this young woman who had learned to depend only on herself. She brought to almost every visit with Pamela a story from a newspaper or magazine about a young person who was able to overcome the worst. "I was so fearful that she would become discouraged," Pat says. The newspaper clippings became a running joke between the two, but Pamela says she has kept every one.

A switch to a strong foster home, the devotion of one passionate CASA volunteer, and Pamela's tenacity put her on a better path toward the end of high school. She has earned a laundry list of scholarships and become a poised and powerful public speaker, taking her insights on the foster care system all the way to the Governor. This fall, Pamela started her freshman year at Oregon State University. She wants to study English, history, and music. James says they will absolutely stay in touch. "I just feel blessed to have had her case."

Hope

I trusted her more with every visit and every call and found myself enjoying her check-ups and questioning. She became not only an advocate, but a friend I could truly count on.

The police arrived to take me away from my family when I was 7 years old. Foster homes came and went. Schools were here and there. Caseworkers drifted in and out of my life. I had just moved from an awful six-year placement with alcoholics when the court appointed me a CASA volunteer.

That summer I had a court hearing, and the judge sent me home. Not to the foster home I had quickly come to love but to my mother. My CASA, Pat, didn't recommend that I go home, and I didn't want to go home, but the judge said, "You are young and you don't know what's best for you."

My mother arrived that night. I opened the door and stood looking at her. I knew she was my mom. I loved her and didn't want to hurt her, but I didn't want her life. I wanted something better for my future.

"I'm not leaving with you," was all I said.

The next morning my caseworker came and demanded I go home with my mom. I entered my mother's apartment and went straight to my room. There was a bed with no blankets, a closet overflowing with trash, and a dresser against one wall. The carpet was littered with cigarette ashes and the entire apartment reeked of smoke, waste, and mildew. I lay down on the mattress and cried.

Pat came to see me quite often and called me when she couldn't come in person. She worked with my lawyer to appeal the court's decision.

Pat was there for me the entire way, advocating for visits with my old foster family, making sure I was seeing my therapist regularly, and checking with my teachers to make sure I was managing in school. She brought me newspaper clippings of youth who made it through hard times and of students who were able to get scholarships to cover their educations. She told me things can only get better, and that I just needed to hang in there 'til they do.

I never had someone stand up for me like she did. She stood before the judge, the lawyers, my mother, and caseworkers and wasn't swayed by their opinions. It completely amazed me. I trusted her more with every visit and every call and found myself enjoying her check-ups and questioning. She became not only an advocate, but a friend I could truly count on.

The summer of my second year home, I went out of town for a night with my best friend. My mom called early the next morning and was yelling before I even had the phone to my ear. Although we had never discussed when I would return, she said she had reported me as a runaway and that the police were coming to take me to juvenile hall. I couldn't believe she would be so crazy!

She was still yelling when I got home so I went straight to my room and locked the door. She stood yelling through it, saying that I had better be packing because the police were on their way. While I stood crying, I noticed something on my shelf—my medications. They couldn't take me if I was dying could they? I grabbed all the pills I could find and some old water from my nightstand and sat on my bed. I heard pounding up the stairs and then on my door.

"I just came to tell you that your sister called the police on you again," my mother growled. "She reported you as a runaway too."

"How can she do that when I am SITTING ON MY OWN BED!" I screamed. "Well," she replied, "if you think someone might run away, you can report it." That was all the push I needed. One by one I began taking the pills. There was knocking on my door again. It was my sister this time.

"Matthew and Albert are here if you want to come down and see them," she said.

"What?! Why would I want to see them?" I yelled at her. "They are not supposed to be ANYWHERE NEAR ME. THE JUDGE SAID SO!!" Those two men were the reason we all had been taken away in the first place. I could not believe she would be so blind.

I started crying. I was so afraid. I didn't really want to die; I just wanted out. That's all. Out. I could only think of one person to call for help. I snuck quietly out of my room, slipped into the next room, and dialed Pat's number. She was calm and steady when she asked questions. She called poison control on her other line, and, as I waited for a response, my mom stormed into the room.

"What are you doing? Calling and telling them what a big, bad mom I am? Well, I have a few things I could tell them…"

I cut her off before she could finish. "No, actually I am talking to Pat who is trying to figure out if the pills I just took are going to kill me," I said evenly.

"I cannot believe this! Get in the car. I'm taking you to the ER right now," she exclaimed.

I sat in the front seat, hardly able to keep my head up, trying to keep the saliva in my mouth, occasionally wiping it with the back of my hand. I couldn't keep my eyes open any longer. I let them close as I swam in the mist, listening to my mother's raving…then, I didn't even hear her.

I was admitted to the hospital immediately and drilled with questions as nurses hooked me up to an IV and stuck wires to my back and chest.

Pat called me the next day and we began to plan what would be my final move. She took care of all the phone calls to the lawyers, the court, and the caseworker. Two weeks later, I moved into my eighth home and since then life has been amazing.

My CASA volunteer is still a big part of my life. She still brings newspaper clippings of youth who have had rough lives. I talk to her often and even visit her at her office now and then. She helped me find money to pay for all of the activities I was involved in senior year, so that I wouldn't have to work all the time and could have, "the best senior year ever," as she said. And I did. I really did.

She was my mentor for my Senior Quest project and even attended my graduation from high school. With her encouragement, I applied for and received scholarships to pay for more than four years of college. I am now an intern at the Oregon Commission on Children and Families, working with the state CASA coordinator on some wonderful projects. I want to make a difference for children still lost in the sea of the child welfare system. I hope to be the change I want to see in the world, as Gandhi once said.

Earlier this week, I was invited with my CASA and a few others to a meeting with the governor. Earlier this year, I testified to a legislative committee on behalf of the CASA program. At the end of the testimony I said; "To give a child a CASA is to give them a voice. To give them a voice is to give them hope, and to give them hope is to give them the world." I believe that with all my heart.

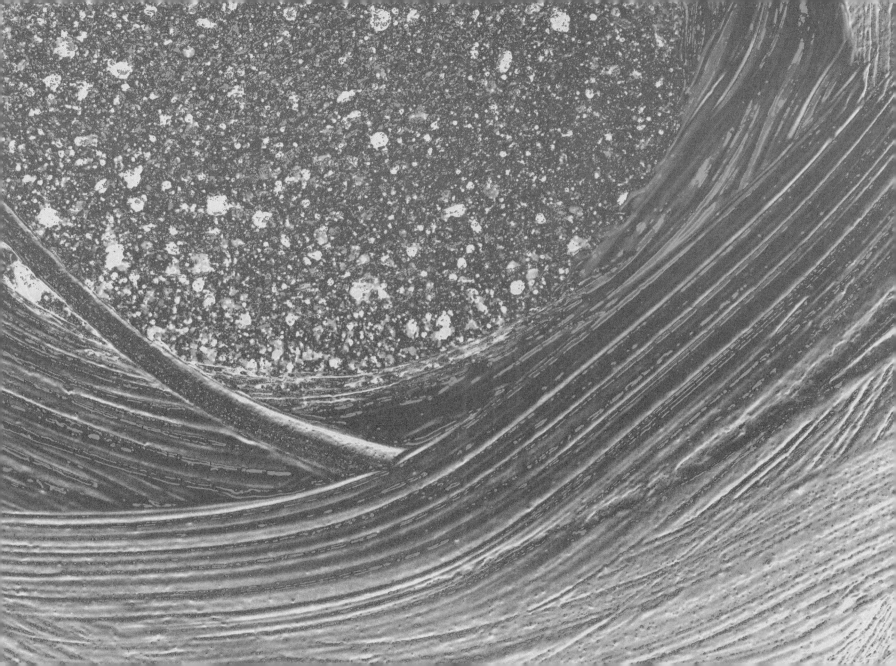

Katie Rosenstein
Cornelius, Oregon
CASA for Children Inc.

"It wasn't until Katie got a CASA volunteer that she realized people cared about what she has to say," says Jennifer Endicott with CASA for Children Inc. in Portland, Oregon. Through watching others advocate for her, Katie Rosenstein became unafraid to stand up for herself, participate in her court hearings, and be downright outspoken. She even pressed to address the crowd at a recent CASA fundraiser. "That's been a big change," says Jennifer.

Before being removed from home, Katie was essentially caring for herself and her autistic brother, washing clothes in the bathtub and trying to keep the household together. Kerry Reynolds was a new CASA volunteer when she was assigned Katie's case. The two clicked. "I just love this girl," says Kerry. She describes Katie as mature and open to new experiences and says she has a great sense of humor and tremendous compassion for others. "Despite all she's been through, she's just a loving, caring person."

Kerry says Katie is now learning to live as part of a family for the first time and has gotten involved in dance classes and a soccer team. "She seems to excel at whatever she does."

Note: In Katie's Essay, the unnamed
"Her" or "She" is Katie's birthmother.

Healing the Heart

Kerry was and still is my security. She is the one I go to when I am having problems. It's very much a wonder to me what foster children did years ago when they didn't have CASAs. I know that I wouldn't have survived court, much less my birthmother, without Kerry, my CASA volunteer.

I'm late again. I'll probably have to talk to a counselor again. It's not like talking with Mrs. Davidian would stop me from waiting up for Her. She is always late. When she is supposed to be home at nine, she is home at three A.M.

Even when Matt and I plead with her to come home on time, she just gallivants off to her other life, leaving us without one.

When she is home, she's either smoking or sleeping. We tell her to quit or it'll rot her teeth, but she ignores our protests. She ignores everything, not even noticing that I have become the mother in the house in exchange for school.

It's not that I don't go to school; it's that I don't pay attention. I'm too tired from waiting up for her. Then I sleep in and am late for first period. I HATE MY LIFE!

I wish my friend Alina never moved away, then life wouldn't be as bad. I could always hide at her house when things went wrong. But she's in Oregon City now, an hour from Tigard, and She never drives me places.

Anyway, back to the present. The office lady said I could go to third period, Mrs. Schnell's reading class.

As I walk in the class, Mrs. Schnell and my homeroom teacher, Mr. Alvarez, motion me over to the desk.

"Kate, you need to do your speech next and then Mr. Alvarez says you have a visitor in the office," says Mrs. Schnell. Mr. Alvarez nods. "Kate, Officer Eskew is here to talk to you," he calmly states.

I nod numbly and walk over to the speech circle to give my speech. When I'm finished, Mr. Alvarez escorts me out of the room and into the office.

A few minutes later, Officer Eskew walks in and asks for me. I jump up, and he tells me we are going for a little ride.

As we walk out to his car, I notice Matt is in the back seat. My heart lurches into my throat as I think of what he might have done now. I close the door as I sit in the car. I can see Mrs. Davidian smiling and waving at me.

What's going on?

That night, our caseworker, Wendy, explained that the police got an anonymous call saying that we might be getting abused. The police came to our apartment to check it out and found Matt, 14, naked and laying in a pile of trash and rat poop. That was enough to send us to foster homes, Wendy explained.

"I'm not sure how long you will be in foster homes, but it won't be for more than a year or so," she finished. That made my day. Even though leaving my family was painful, I wanted a better life. As it ended up, I was put with a great foster mom, Sally.

In March of 2002, I was granted a CASA volunteer, Kerry, but I didn't need her in court until I moved away from Sally. While I was with Sally, Kerry was just my best friend and confidante. When I told Her that I didn't want to live with her anymore, Kerry was there to support me, and guide me to my goals. She was my shoulder to cry on.

In August 2002, I moved to another foster home. The Monroes were and are great advocates for their children, but, being foster parents, they are limited. Cindy Monroe, my mom, guided my caseworker and attorney to a permanency hearing, while Kerry guided me to my goals and gave me advice. She also guided mom through the process of permanency when my caseworker was "temporarily unavailable."

Kerry was and still is my security. She is the one I go to when I am having problems. From the start of our relationship, she was the only one I felt comfortable telling everything. For some people, the changing situation was hard to deal with and they took it out on me. Then, I would vent to Kerry. She never minded it. She would just talk me through it and tell me how wonderful and amazing I am, giving me smiles and encouraging me to start my dreams and face the world.

She and Jen, her supervisor, arranged for me to speak at a CASA fundraiser, with my permission. We recorded my speech and they played it at the formal dinner. Here is a portion of it: "Seven out of 13 children, neglected and abused, get a CASA. But all 13 need a CASA. Kids like me, we need compliments and smiles to help us through the hard times. We need guidance and support. All 13 of us."

I don't know what I'd ever do without Kerry. I love her dearly, and I am very glad that she came into my life.

I just registered as an advice giver at a website for abused or hurt teens. I read their stories and see how they are hurt and need help. Then I try to give them advice in a way they will understand. I learned to do that from Kerry. And for that, I am very thankful.

Once I am old enough to qualify and am ready I am going to become either a foster parent or CASA volunteer or travel around and tell my story. I hope that, somehow, it'll reach the kids who really need it.

Karla Sanchez
San Diego, California
Voices for Children San Diego

Karla Sanchez, a former foster child, is a young woman who is accustomed to taking care of everyone but herself. The oldest of three girls, she was often responsible for her siblings—sometimes taking care of them instead of going to school. "She's usually the first person to comfort someone else or to hold someone's hand," says Sabrina Goosby, the director of volunteers with Voices for Children San Diego. "She's always the one who's the giver."

In her essay, Karla says she was surprised that her CASA volunteer, Kim Koenigs, would choose to take time from her full schedule and spend it with her. But Kim was stubborn and willing to give Karla all the time she needed. CASA program supervisor Briana Ogletree says Karla would not have graduated from high school were it not for Kim. She would sit for hours with Karla in her dirty, crowded foster home and help her with homework assignments. On the day of Karla's graduation, Kim brought her into the CASA office so everyone could acknowledge her accomplishment.

Now 20, Karla has stayed closely involved with Voices for Children San Diego, working with Briana in an aftercare program and participating in "Real Word" panels to educate the community about youth in foster care. Briana says Karla is gaining confidence, learning to speak up for herself, asking for help when she needs it, and making herself more of a priority. Maybe someone just needed to convince her she was worth it.

Kim and I

A week before my prom, Kim and I went to search for a dress. It was so special for me that she was by my side because I wished my mom had been with me in those moments. I picked a magenta dress that had diamonds around the top and a fluffy bottom.

The first time I met my CASA volunteer, Kim, I was thinking, how can she help me and take time for me when she could be doing things for herself? I also wondered why would she want to help me when I didn't have any one who cared about me? Before she came into my life I had a really nice social worker, but I didn't have a good foster mother. I had many problems with my foster mother. She never supported me and was not involved in my education. In addition, I was only 17 and she wanted me to be just like her. She would also complain that I had behavior problems, but in my heart I know I was doing my best to do everything right. The only thing I wanted was someone who would be there for me, be supportive, and not criticize me.

Before I met my CASA, Kim, I was failing all my classes and was not expected to graduate on time. Kim immediately started to help me with my education. She would come to see me once a week. She would make sure I was doing my homework and studying. One night we spent hours reviewing what I needed to know for my senior year English test.

Even though Kim and I studied, the next day I took my test and forgot a lot of what we talked about, and I didn't pass. I had to go to night school to pass my English class in order to graduate. In my second semester, I passed my English class with an A. I wish you could have seen Kim's expression when I gave her the good news.

My CASA would organize appointments with everyone who was involved in my life: my therapist, social worker, foster mom, and case manager. She made sure that everyone was doing what was necessary to help me succeed. Everybody thought I was not going to graduate so Kim would also call my counselor to hear how I was doing in my classes. While I was completing my senior year, my only dream was graduating with my class.

My CASA said that I was working so hard that I deserved to have fun and participate in the senior activities. She convinced me to go to prom. A week before my prom, Kim and I went to search for a dress. It was so special for me that she was by my side because I wished my mom had been with me in those moments. I picked a magenta dress that had diamonds around the top and a fluffy bottom. I still have memories about my prom thanks to her. If I had not gone to the prom, I know I would have regretted it.

My CASA volunteer not only helped with my education, she would always call me to see how I was doing. Because of her, I got to see my sisters more often than I had before. She made sure I got to visit my sisters' foster homes. I was so happy every time I got to see my sisters. That showed me that Kim was really there for me and cared about my happiness.

Kim also helped me get into Trolley Trestle, a transitional living program. She and I would get together or talk on the phone to see how the process was going. She didn't like where I lived because the foster home was filthy and didn't support or encourage me in any way. Kim thought I should move into a better place where I could take care of myself and be independent. There was only one problem, I had to be emancipated and my new social worker was procrastinating on contacting my attorney. Kim had to call my attorney and talk to other people to schedule the court hearing. When I finally moved to Trolley Trestle, Kim and I went to Target where she helped me pick out some things for my apartment. I was so happy that I had someone to accompany me, because I didn't have any family support. I was proud that she got to see my achievement.

From the time I turned 6 until now, I have helped my mother take care of my younger sisters. Since I have been in the foster care system, I've been able to help other foster kids. I try to support them and tell them where they can get help. For the past year, I have been on a speakers' panel, The Real Word, through Voices for Children. By being on the panel, I get the opportunity to give the new CASAs ideas about how to understand a teenager in foster care. I have also had the chance to speak to foster parents, group home staff and residents, and community groups. I enjoy helping other kids in the system and educating others on foster care issues. The panel provides me with support and encouragement. Sharing my experiences has helped me deal with all that I've been through. I am currently attending city college and want to be a social worker.

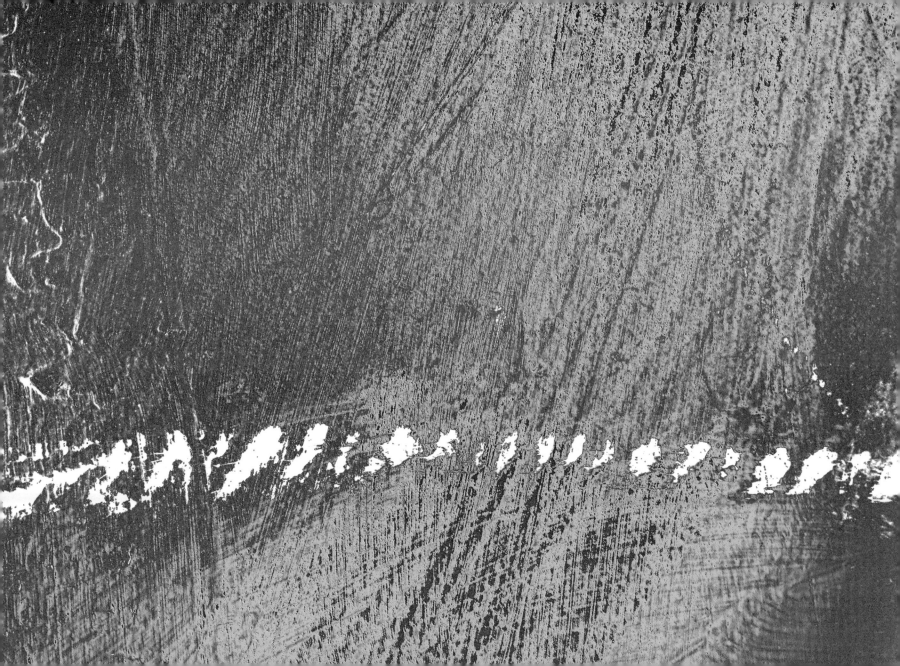

Amber Snyder
Newton, North Carolina
Guardian ad Litem, 25th Judicial District of North Carolina

Peter West took on the case of Amber Snyder in 1999. Amber was the oldest of three siblings and certainly the caretaker, says Peter. "She had to make sure her brothers got what they needed."

Peter describes Amber as an intelligent, energetic, and exuberant young woman with a tender spirit. He says she was driven and grounded by the successes she achieved in school, band, and her ROTC program.

Although Peter says there were some battles in Amber's case, the system worked effectively to move Amber and her brothers into a permanent placement with their paternal grandmother. Peter says it is an example of what can happen when there's strong advocacy.

That advocacy left Amber with a relatively good feeling about her time in the child welfare system and a positive attitude about all she's faced. "It made me able to deal with things because I've had to rise above and be strong," she says. Amber is settling into her freshman year at the University of North Carolina, Charlotte, and is strongly considering going into social work.

Peter says he thinks Amber was deeply affected by seeing other kids in need as she and her brothers made their way through the system. As a result, she found ways to reach out to other young people in care. Angela Phillips, the district administrator, recalls Amber's case as one of the system's too-rare happy endings. She says, "We have to hang on to the Amber stories."

My GAL

I will never be able to repay my GAL.
He knew I needed to be treated like I was somebody important.

Have you ever had the only world you've known pulled right out from under your feet? Four and a half years ago, that is exactly what happened to me. It was the scariest thing I had ever witnessed, and it was happening to me.

I had given up on my real parents' ability to provide a safe and secure life for me. I felt a need that was not being met, and God guided me to someone who could help. I was placed in the safe care of the state of North Carolina. At that time, I felt unloved by my parents and alone in school. All my friends still lived with their "real" families, but I didn't. I was, however, very grateful to be out of the chaotic life my birthfamily created.

After coming into care, I was introduced to a man who said he would be my "GAL." I found that weird because he was a man. I later found out what GAL stood for, guardian ad litem. He is a wonderful man. Was and still is my Guardian Angel Legally, my GAL. He and his coworkers worked really hard to help me get what I needed. When all the other support teams couldn't help with my needs and issues, the whole GAL system built the bridge to meet my needs and resolve my issues. The time that sticks out in my mind most was the summer after my eighth grade year. The Beta Club was going on a reward trip to Carowinds theme park. I really wanted to go, but we didn't have the money to spare. We spoke to my social worker, and he couldn't help me with the money. We also spoke to the GAL program. They said they would see what they could do. In the end, my GAL brought me the money for my trip. I later found out that he took up a collection at the office so I could go on my trip. That is one of the many special things the GAL program has done for me. Any time we went to court, my GAL would make a point to find out what I wanted and how I felt and carried my voice to the judge. They also helped my grandmother, whom I call mom, to adopt me and my two brothers. My GAL never made me feel like I was just a case or a number. He always made me feel that what I had to say was important and really mattered. I will never be able to repay my GAL. He knew I needed to be treated like I was somebody important.

The summer after my freshman year, I was given the opportunity to do an internship with the GAL office. I really enjoyed learning more about their program and how they work with people. I had the privilege of filing papers, making copies, and rearranging the filing cabinets and was given the high honor of being trusted with confidentiality. That summer was truly a learning experience, and I will always be grateful for the opportunity extended to me by my GAL.

My mom has always taught us to give back and be thankful for those who have helped us. One year, Mom said, "We're going to do something special for some people this Christmas." My brothers and I, with the help of my mom, decided to use our saved allowance to buy small gifts for children. We also collected some of our stuffed animals to bring other children comfort. We wrapped the gifts in brightly colored cellophane paper, put them in the car, and took them all to the GAL office. The look on their faces made me cry. They were so surprised and glad to have the little gifts to give children who were in care. It felt so good to support the cause of such a wonderful and caring agency. My GAL was so grateful and excited to receive our gifts for the children. That moment changed my life forever. The warmness of giving far exceeds the joy of receiving.

The next year, I decided to make a bigger project. Just a few teddy bears would not be enough to meet the needs of children in crisis. I went to my student council director and proposed the idea to collect teddy bears for children in crisis as our Christmas project. The director was so excited she had me introduce the idea at our next meeting. I explained that the stuffed animals are given to children when they come into care and stay with them wherever they go. Sometimes when a child comes into care, he or she has nothing. If they are given a stuffed animal that is soft and cozy, they will feel more comfortable and secure.

My motion passed unanimously. Our plan was to collect stuffed animals for a week or two before Christmas break. I would deliver the stuffed animals to the GAL office. Our slogan for the teddy bear drive was: "Please bring in a new or old stuffed animal for a child in crisis to be used as a transitional object, to be taken from place to place."

The student body loved the idea, and the drive was a huge success! We collected more than 300 stuffed animals! I was shocked at the amount! I knew that would be too many to give to the GAL program. I discussed it with my mom. She suggested I give some to social services so they could also give a child in crisis a transitional object. Again, when I made the deliveries, the looks on the faces of the GALs brought tears to my eyes. I plan to continue the tradition of giving. I am grateful to all those who taught me the precious lesson to give with all your heart.

Thank you "My GAL" and everyone who has helped me get to where I am today. You are my heroes!

Elizabeth Velasquez
Merrimac, Massachusetts

Elizabeth Velasquez is pure teenager. With the rapid-fire speech of a Northerner and abundant energy, the 17-year-old will cover her life story in mere minutes, often lacing a giggle through her sentences. She loves the movies, hanging out with boys, doing hair, and shopping. And she has big dreams to go on to college and possibly become a doctor or a lawyer.

"She has a smile that lights up a room," says Tracey Walden, Elizabeth's CASA volunteer since 2000, "just a gorgeous, gleaming smile that everyone comments on."

Although typically upbeat and positive, Elizabeth can also be startlingly frank and honest, revealing the world wisdom of a young woman who has been through too much. During her preteen years Elizabeth says she was being sexually abused by her mother's boyfriend during weekend visits home. One morning her grandmother noticed a change in Elizabeth's normally wiry frame and took her to the doctor. She was already six months along and not yet even 13.

Tracey says she and Elizabeth just felt an instant fondness for one another. "I've helped her with school and when she's had hard times," Tracy says, "just talking and being there for her." One of the things Tracey worked with Elizabeth on was expressing how she was feeling and asking for help when she needed it. Elizabeth says that Tracey helped her learn that she didn't have to tell people only what they wanted to hear.

Tracey marvels at Elizabeth's optimism and resilience. "She's going to struggle maybe, but she's an emotionally tough person," says Tracey. She also says Elizabeth is an incredibly hard worker in school and has almost always had a part-time job. Right now she's working at a nearby fast food restaurant after school. Tracey believes Elizabeth's willingness to work hard and her desire to do right are going to get her wherever she wants to go. "She's going to make it," Tracey says, "thanks to no one but herself." Elizabeth, however, has a slightly different take on who has helped her through.

My Life Savior

I never had someone to care about the little things in my life before—or even the big things!

For the past four years I have been fortunate to have Tracey Walden as my guardian ad litem. Through those years, Tracey has inspired me in many different ways. She helped me to find myself within. She taught me to be myself and not to put on an act for other people. Because of Tracey's interest in my life, she made me feel special. She spent a lot of time searching for good homes and placements for me that would match my interests. When I didn't like a placement, Tracey would acknowledge my feelings, yet also encourage me to hold on and get through it. She reassured me that I had something to look forward to because someday I would have a stable home environment and people to care about me. Tracey was someone who brought the sadness in my life to joy. She always told me that everything would get better when I worried about my life.

When I first met Tracey, I was having a very rough time. I was 12 years old and about six months pregnant. I had been violated by my mother's boyfriend. I was a very worried child and thought that being raped had been my fault. I was feeling very unwanted and Tracey was my only hope. She turned things around and made me feel wanted by offering me comfort and support. She assured me that it was not my fault. She used to worry about my grades in school, how I was doing at my placements, and other little aspects of my life. This made me feel SO GOOD because I never had someone to care about the little things in my life before—or even the big things! She was there when I decided to give the baby I had up for adoption, and continued to offer her support unconditionally throughout the years.

I had been yearning for someone to talk to and to share my feelings with when Tracey was appointed to me. Her presence in my life was an enormous help. Of course, I did not realize all of this at the time. Now, when I think back to how much she helped me in my life during some very difficult times, I see how my successes are greatly related to her assistance and gentle, unending guidance.

Tracey's influence in my life has enabled me to move on and to help other girls I have come to know. The girls who I lived with in a program for parenting teens would regularly bicker about how the Department of Social Services had made their lives living hells. One day I decided to offer my input. I told them that if it wasn't for the system there was a chance that half of us would be dead. I then began to tell my life story. I shared that I had no father, no one to care for me like I needed, and how I was raped. I told them to look into that predicament and tell me they would want to live at home rather than in a safe environment. I really had those girls thinking and I mean hard! Some of them even began to cry. From that time on, I began to see a slight change in the girls.

They say that you cannot love another unless you first love yourself. I also believe that you cannot help another unless you first help yourself. Because of Tracey Walden, I have been able to do both and my life is now more fulfilling. Tracey has been my life savior.

Najiba A.
Fairfax CASA, Virginia

Najiba A., 16, has covered huge distances in her life: from the Ivory Coast of Africa to the horse country of Virginia, and from a scared young girl who wouldn't even make eye contact to a bright, musical teen who is adjusting to a new foster home and a new school.

For her first case as a CASA volunteer, Rachel Knapik would drive an hour to see Najiba in her group home. She says Najiba's face just showed how much she had been through. Rachel supported Najiba during her time in the group home, and, about a year into the case, a teacher came forward and asked to serve as a foster parent for Najiba. Rachel says that because the advocacy aspects of the case were pretty straightforward, her main focus was to offer Najiba support and comfort. "She really just needed someone to be there," Rachel says.

Rachel is in her 20s, and Najiba felt that her volunteer's age helped her relate well to her and trust her. "She just had a lot of strange adults in her life," Rachel says. It was a relief to her to have someone with whom she was really comfortable. And Najiba clearly made an impression on Rachel; "I just think the world of her," she says.

My CASA Worker

A single visit from my CASA worker means the world to me.
Having her there just to talk to keeps me from crashing to that low point in my life.

Words alone can not express my feelings of having a CASA worker. Spending time and even talking to her alone has been a wonderful experience for me. The amount of energy and care she put into helping me succeed in life has been incredible.

I live in a residential placement, and, sometimes, or should I say often, I have emotional breakdowns. These breakdowns are often caused by stress and anxiety, which causes me to isolate in the quiet room. Well, a few months ago I had an emotional breakdown and was in a hole too deep to get out of. That afternoon, I was supposed to have a class off grounds with my CASA worker, but I wasn't in a situation where I could leave the premises. My CASA worker came, and, instead of arranging another pass for another week, she stayed in the quiet room and talked to me. My CASA worker helped me see that there are a ton of people who care for and support me. She spent at least two hours visiting and talking to me, and, during that time, I could tell she

wasn't very comfortable in such a small place. But she stayed and helped me get out of the hole I thought was impossible to get out of.

My CASA worker is extremely devoted to what she does, and I can tell by the way she has shown up to every single court date, even the ones that were just five minutes long. I don't get many visits here because my parents don't have custody of me. A single visit from my CASA worker means the world to me. Having her there just to talk to keeps me from crashing to that low point in my life. During court, I often feel anxious and upset, but my CASA worker holds me and assures me that I won't be harmed by my father.

Whenever I am not sure of what decisions to make, I often think of what my CASA worker would think or say and I do it. She has never asked much of me, only to feel free to express my feelings and be myself around her. From my experiences with my CASA worker, I have learned to be more understanding of others. Whenever the residents of my facility feel upset, I usually refrain from giving advice, but I always give my support and sympathy. Whenever they feel like cutting, running, or doing something to regress their treatment I tell them what my CASA worker would tell me. I tell them that if they harm themselves, their loving and caring family and friends would be devastated.

Because of my great experiences with my CASA worker and other people who have been a wonderful part of my life, I have been encouraged to give back to the community. I hope to someday take an active part in the foster care system and maybe show someone else that there are wonderful benefits in living and loving yourself.

Thank you Rachel for giving me back my life.

Sonia Aguilar
Santa Cruz, California
CASA of Santa Cruz

"Eileen has one of those quiet, persistent voices," says CASA of Santa Cruz Executive Director Susan True of volunteer Eileen Hodson. "She just won't stop until she gets what her CASA child needs."

When Eileen was assigned as an advocate for Sonia Aguilar and her younger sister, the girls had been recently removed from their parents and placed in an unsafe foster home. Eileen voiced her concerns, and voiced them again and again, until she got the girls moved. When the sisters both needed orthodontic care that was too pricey for the state to cover, Eileen found a local orthodontist who was happy to provide a deeply discounted rate. She then continued to request that the state cover the procedures until both girls were in braces. And as she was working to find ways to bring the sisters out of their shells a bit, Eileen discovered their interest in dance. She asked around until she found a studio willing to provide free lessons for them. "She just got those resources," Susan says, "And found support and generosity in the community."

Eileen also worked with Sonia to help the bright girl fill the gaps in her education and graduate from high school. "As a goal-oriented and intelligent young woman, it was easy to encourage Sonia to make her education a priority," says Eileen. Sonia is now working part-time and attending a local community college with the goal to go on to nursing school. The cheery, positive teen, long the caregiver in the family, also works very hard at keeping her siblings in touch.

When she aged out of care at 18, Sonia decided she really wanted to help get more CASA volunteers for kids and agreed to speak at a CASA membership luncheon. When Sonia mentioned that she liked to write, one of the volunteers in attendance told her she could help her place an article with the local paper.

The piece reprinted here originally appeared in the Santa Cruz Sentinel, and Sonia's powerful words did exactly what the thoughtful teen had hoped. Susan says, "I can't tell you how many people have come to us to become a volunteer and said, 'I've been thinking about doing this since I read that young woman's story.'"

Reprinted with permission from the Santa Cruz Sentinel, *Santa Cruz, California.*

Seeing Life in a New Way

Suddenly, it seemed a part of my life was ripped out from the ground I stood on, and it was hard for me to stand tall. I was only 14, and I felt the weight of the world on my shoulders. It hurt even more to know that my brothers and sisters were going through the same pain.

I remember when it started like it was yesterday. The touch, the feel, the smell, the sight and sound of those crazy days. It was when the sun still burned bright and hot, warming up everything in its path from the tallest buildings to the smallest creatures, casting small black shadows over everything it touched and making the earth on the ground seem like a cartoon of black figures.

It was a time when everything seemed all right, even if just for that moment in time. And change...change was a good thing then. It was a time, I guess, that I lived in a bubble of fantasies, old enough to know what good and evil were, but too young to understand why such things happened.

Soon reality would burst my bubble, and I would finally realize what life was really about. I'm the oldest of seven children. We almost took care of ourselves. Having to grow up so fast led me into the adult world of thinking about responsibility. Things such as abuse, drugs, alcohol, poverty, and neglect lead to the destruction of a family. Yes, I admit that some of those things were the cause of the separation of my family, but the others were from the point of view of the Child Protective Services system.

Every child wants to believe that their family is normal and as good as everyone else's. With all that was going on at that point, I knew something would happen. I felt it beneath my skin. I just didn't know what or when. Eventually the system got involved in our lives, and before we knew it, we were separated into different homes. Suddenly, it seemed a part of my life was ripped out from the ground I stood on, and it was hard for me to stand tall. I was only 14, and I felt the weight of the world on my shoulders. It hurt even more to know that my brothers and sisters were going through the same pain.

Everybody told us it would be a couple of weeks in foster care but it turned into months, then years. There are good homes and bad. It depends on the people under that roof. I ended up with a person that I can't say was bad, because everybody has a heart. I guess she didn't know how to treat kids that weren't her own.

Overwhelmed with depression, loneliness, and hopelessness, I started thinking about suicide as an option. I didn't want to wake up in the morning, and I was mad at the world. It was as if now I was forced to be different.

As the months went by, I saw my mom fall deeper and deeper into a hole of depression. I was sad because the only person I looked up to for strength and protection had given up. Imagine what a mother goes through after losing her children, doing everything she can to get them back, but still failing. That feeling of hopelessness led her to become homeless. It was then that I was a true believer of the fact that life has a way of taking you places you never imagined.

As the oldest child, I felt a great responsibility to bring my family back together and make everything better again, yet there were so many things holding me down. My dad was able to get my youngest brother, and again, I realized that love conquers hate. In the past, I never respected him; now I'm thankful he never gave up.

Suddenly, a new person walked into the lives of my sister and me.

With the constant changing of social worker and counselors, I didn't know what to expect. This woman introduced herself as Eileen Hodson, a CASA. I had never heard of this. She asked us what our interests were, and we set up a time to meet every week. I felt that this just might be a good thing.

As the weeks went by, we got to know each other better. I realized that I could talk to her about problems, not only personal problems, but problems about the homes we lived in. She was our voice, my stability, and a friend. A lot of people might want to help children, but think to themselves, "What difference would I make?"

The truth is that there are not enough CASAs for every broken child. Not only did my relationship with my CASA help me grow and prosper; it turned into a lifelong relationship. She may not have even realized her impact on my life because she was simply just being a friend. Someone you can talk to, and someone you can trust. It's the simple things that make someone complete as a person.

Now I'm 18, going to college and have a job, a stage in my life I seriously believed I would not live to see. I thank God for keeping me strong and letting me live to see a brighter day. I can't say that I would take back any part of my life because it has made me the person I am today. Thank you Eileen, for being that someone. And I hope, someday, I'll help someone in my situation see life in a brand new way.

Cortney Blanton
Spring, Texas
Child Protective Services Harris County/Child Advocates, Inc.

Cortney Blanton was only 11 years old when she was faced with the painful and nerve-wracking task of testifying against a member of her own family in front of a judge, lawyers, and a courtroom of people. The young girl was understandably scared.

Cortney's caseworker, Tamara Petty-Anderson, worked with Cortney to get her more comfortable with what she had to do. Tamara brought Cortney to the courthouse and even let her spend time in the courtroom and meet some of its staff. But Tamara says it was still difficult to get Cortney over the fear of having the lawyers question her in front of so many people. It was ultimately Tamara's advice to Cortney to have faith in the truth she had to tell that got the young girl through the experience. Cortney showed how brave and strong she could be on her day in court, just as she had on the day she went to a school administrator about what was happening at home.

Some friends of the family, whom Cortney calls her aunt and uncle, came forward to provide a home for Cortney and her sister after Cortney's revelation. CASA volunteer Laura Wirth says she worked with Tamara and the couple to get them permanent custody of the girls. The couple was eager to have the sisters and willing to take the extra step to go through the 10-week course to become certified foster parents. Laura says the arrangement provides the girls with the security of a home, but still gives their "aunt and uncle" help with the unexpected costs of two more teens in their home and eventually two more college students.

Tamara says Cortney is a personable young girl with an easy smile and an impressive drive to succeed in school. The high school freshman is on the honor roll and involved in drama. Although she has been through some incredibly difficult situations, Cortney was lucky to have supportive adults and some good advice to help her through it all.

Ms. Petty's Advice

As I was getting settled in to my new home, I heard I had to go to court. I was devastated. I couldn't do that. I was only 11 years old.

Have you ever heard your mom or dad say; "Listen to this little advice it may help you someday?" I couldn't understand how criticism or critiquing could help me. But Tamara Petty-Anderson, my Child Protective Services (CPS) worker turned that all around when I needed advice most on July 9, 2002.

You may want to know what was going on that day I needed advice. It all dates back to when a problem that had been happening for three years ended on May 11, 2002. I went to the assistant principal at F.M. Black Middle School to tell the horrifying story. She quickly dialed CPS to report what had been happening at my home. One or two hours later, Ms. Sally was at my school to pick me up and take me to CPS. I was a little afraid of what might happen to me. As soon as I got there I was taken to get an interview. It wasn't as bad as I thought it would be. After 30 minutes of interviewing, I was taken into a little office to see what would happen next. About an hour later my sister came in to tell me that our uncle would not be taking us home until Tuesday. The weekend quickly passed by. My sister and I were soon taken to a group home called Lamar Village to stay, but about a week later we were back at my aunt and uncle's house.

As I was getting settled in to my new home, I heard I had to go to court. I was devastated. I couldn't do that. I was only 11 years old. Months went by with no notice of when I was going to court. After one year, I was 12 at this time, I found out that my lawyer, Cary, had finally set a date of July 9, 2002. I grew more scared as each day passed. Finally, I met Ms. Petty, my CPS worker. She was the nicest person I ever knew. Ms. Petty sat and talked to me about how court actually worked, and I got a brown teddy bear during my visit to the court building. I named her Petty. I started to ease up a little on the stress of having to go to court. My aunt went out to buy nice clothes for me to wear to court. The days went by so fast I couldn't believe that the next day I had to go.

The next morning, July 9, I was so scared as I put on my red dress with white flowers, but I remembered the teddy bear the court had given me. I quickly swept it off my floor and started hugging the bear for comfort. "Time to go Cortney," my aunt exclaimed. I slowly walked down the stairs of our house to have time to think. We finally arrived at the Harris County courthouse. It was like a maze trying to find my lawyer. I went through metal detectors. I tried to find the right door. I got confused. Finally arriving at the correct spot, I saw Cary and Ms. Petty there waiting for me. Ms. Petty looked at me and could tell I wasn't doing so well, "Cortney, are you feeling alright?" I heard her ask. I looked into her eyes and told her it was impossible for me to do this, I was too scared. Ms. Petty told me to sit down and listen to her. "Cortney, God knows you're telling the truth. You just tell the jury what you know." I realized that Ms. Petty was right. My time drew near to going on the stand to testify. Ms. Petty and I were talking about music, dancing, and movies to keep us occupied. A lady with long blonde hair came into the room. "Cortney, they're ready for you," the tall blonde said. I stood up pale as a sheet and started to quickly walk to the stand. The stand got closer, and I felt my ankles get weak. "Cortney, will you please raise your right hand," the judge asked. "Do you swear to tell the truth, the whole truth and nothing but the truth so help you God?" I stared and her and finally made my reply. I sat down in the chair behind the stand. Cary started off with the questions. I answered her with a little faith. But when they began asking questions I got scared, but I remembered what Ms. Petty told me. "God knows you're telling the truth. You just have to tell the jury what you know." My faith rose a little higher than before. Every answer was given thought before speaking; every question was taken into consideration before I spoke. Sure, I was scared

at first, but thinking about Ms. Petty's words gave me courage and wisdom. I won, not by lying but by being the better person. I didn't have to lie to tell my story. God was on my side leading me down the right path.

It may sound dumb, but until you experience it you have no idea what happened to me on that stand. I'm still thinking of a way I could help kids like me when they have to testify. I want to be able to tell people how it feels and the obstacles you go through.

Danielle Bush
Rochester, New York
CASA of Monroe County

Danielle Bush had just turned 7 when CASA volunteer Elaine Marchetti took her case. The young girl had been in the foster care system since the age of 3, and was the only one of her five siblings to be placed in care.

Elaine thought this hurt little girl had enough social workers and therapists probing into her life already. "I figured my role was to develop a trusting relationship with her and not to be another person who was just asking questions," says Elaine.

As the two began to get to know one other, Elaine says she noticed something exceptional in Danielle. "She had thoughts beyond her age," Elaine explains, "and a deep quality about her." Elaine encouraged Danielle to start putting her thoughts on paper, and Danielle says it was a letter to her first foster family that just wound up taking the form of poetry. Danielle continued writing and, although she was initially reluctant to show her work to others, she soon found a powerful reason to let others read her words. "I've been in foster care for almost 14 years," she says. "I like to help inspire other people to not give up."

Elaine says she thinks it took her several years to earn Danielle's confidence; "She began to trust me as a person who could set some wheels in motion." Elaine says that during Danielle's years at home and in the foster care system she learned people didn't always tell her the truth, so Elaine strove to be as frank and honest as possible as she helped Danielle through different situations. She said it was a turning point when Danielle turned to her one day and told her, 'I can always believe you.'

Elaine's work as a CASA has been acknowledged with awards from the Monroe County office and with less official accolades. Linda Garrison of Kidspeace, the foster care agency through which Danielle was most recently placed, says Elaine brings the kind of information and insight that no case file could ever contain. Danielle simply says, "I know I can always get to her."

Elaine made a promise to Danielle when she was 8 years old that she would stay with her, no matter what, until her 18th birthday. Danielle is now 17 and despite many moves is on track to graduate high school on time. Elaine is battling cancer, but she remains focused on her promise to Danielle. She says, "I made a commitment, and if there ever was a child who needed someone to trust it was Danielle. Whenever she needs me, I am there for her."

Elaine Marchetti died in November 2003.

An Angel of CASA

A Special person who was with me from beginning to end,

during hard times her heart she would lend,

for all the good times her love she would send,

she is a CASA volunteer as well as a friend.

NO Longer being ignored, she was my voice they heard,

always making promises and stuck by her word,

a broken heart for her was nothing to cure.

GIVEN a tough situation she was the one I called

I trusted in her because I knew she had what it took to get it solved.

EXTRAORDINARY is not powerful enough to describe her ambition,

all CASA volunteers open their hearts and set out on a mission.

LOVE is in the heart of those who help a child in need,

to give your time and heart to someone you just meet,

is like being able to pick a flower that you planted as a seed.

Note: This poem was commissioned by the National CASA Association for use in this book. Danielle also wrote a poem featured in Lighting the Way *(the CASA book produced in 1999).*

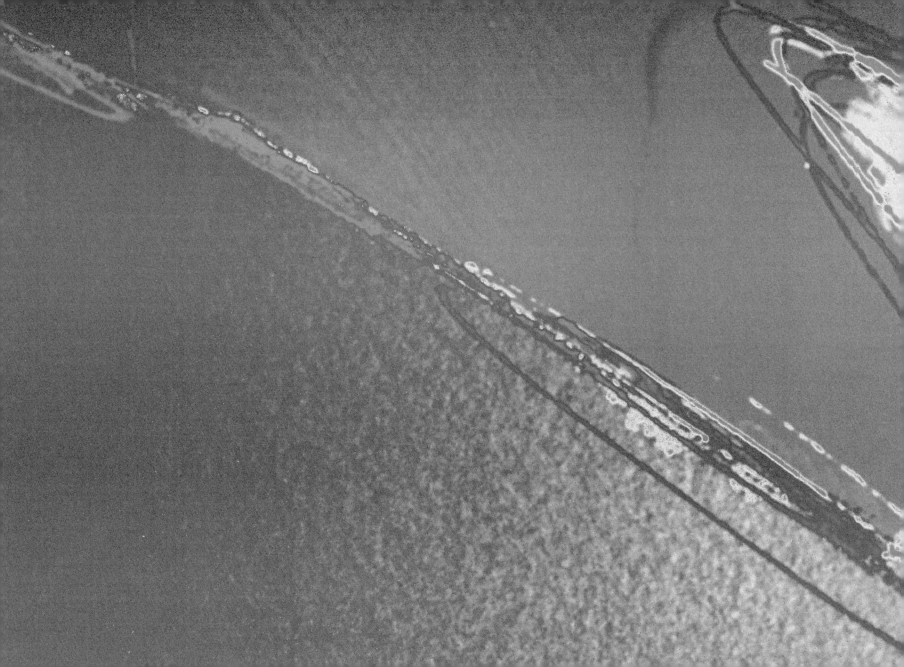

Lerrion G. Byrd and Pam Archie Byrd
Lincoln, Texas
Travis County CASA

Brothers Lerrion and Pam Byrd were 15 and 14 when first-time CASA volunteer Emily Schroeder went to meet them in their foster home. Both boys remember the smile on Emily's face and a quality about her that put them at ease.

Emily's smile and nature are things that come up quickly when people talk about her. Travis County CASA Director Karen Cox calls Emily an amazing force and says that smile stays on her face all the time. "You're not around Emily without knowing you're in the presence of someone special," Karen says.

Lerrion and Pam were initially in a high level of care when they entered the system, but Emily says the boys didn't need really intensive therapy and supervision. They just needed some long overdue stability in their lives. The boys had been living on the streets, in cars, and in shelters. With their older siblings, they would often skip school and spend the afternoon in different corners and underpasses in Austin. "At that point, they had some serious truancy issues," says Emily. "They maybe went to school four or five times in a term." Emily quickly learned that the boys weren't staying away from school because they didn't want to be there but because they were missing the clean clothes and the warm meals and the support that would allow them to make school a priority.

Once the brothers spent some time in a stable setting and got some encouragement from Emily, both boys began to thrive. Emily says she wrote a note in a Christmas card to Lerrion that said she was proud of him. It was what the young man had been waiting to hear. "They started setting goals for their own lives and really focusing on their education," Emily says.

At 18, Lerrion aged out of care and gained entrance into Texas A&M University–Commerce. Emily says he worked and saved up enough money to buy a very used car to take to college. "It had some issues," Emily says about the vehicle. She had a friend look at the car before Lerrion left on the four and a half hour drive to Commerce, Texas. The combination of a bad alternator on the car and Emily's memories of having her mom help her off to college convinced Emily she should caravan behind Lerrion as he drove to school. His car died 30 minutes from campus. Emily helped Lerrion get his stuff to campus only to learn that the deposit for his dorm room hadn't come through. Emily stayed until everything was sorted out and Lerrion's car was in working order. During the ordeal, Lerrion turned to Emily and told her, "If you hadn't been here, I would have just gone back home."

Emily's only lingering concern was that with Lerrion at school, Pam would lose his directional beacon to some extent. The opposite has been true. Pam spends several hours a day on the bus just to get to school and then from school to his part-time job. He has also followed Lerrion's lead into a leadership role in the Texas independent living program.

Emily says some people may think that what she has done as a CASA volunteer is noteworthy, but she sees real heroes when she looks at Lerrion and Pam.

A Positive Future

By Lerrion G. Byrd

One breezy winter evening, my younger brother and I were told we had company.
We heard the loud, jolly voice from our room halfway across the house.
It was Emily Schroeder, and she was our CASA volunteer.

Fear, pain, and sorrow are some of the feelings experienced by young children and adolescent youth who enter the foster care system. Hello, my name is Lerrion G. Byrd, and I am a foster youth who has experienced the elation of having a Court Appointed Special Advocate to help me and my siblings with the transition of coming into the Texas foster care system.

It was the winter of 2000 when my other siblings and I entered the system. My younger brother and I were put in a rural area 65 miles east of Austin, while my older sister was placed in Round Rock, Texas. Of course, we were angry and upset—not only at ourselves, but at the people who separated us from what we thought was our life. My high level of care showed the fury and distress that seemed to frequently take control of my every thought, but only time, or so I thought, could take the pain away.

One breezy winter evening, my younger brother and I were told that we had company. We heard the loud, jolly voice from our room halfway across the house. It was Emily Schroeder, and she was *our*

CASA volunteer. From that day on, our ride to a more recovered and positive life began.

I began to enjoy this away-from-home experience and take advantage of the things that were offered to me through the system. From attending Leadership Conferences to advocating in front of boards of directors, these are the things that I began to get involved in thanks to the support and understanding of my CASA volunteer.

I can remember evenings and afternoons of sheer pleasure and "off time." I can also remember days that Emily came out, all the way from Austin, just to spend time with us—sometimes to sit outside in the evening breeze and just discuss our weeks and weekends.

Although life began to look up for my siblings and me, there were still lingering aggravations and obstacles that seemed to creep up from the embers of our past. But Emily was always there. From the beginning to the end our CASA always seemed to care about our feelings and emotions and not what recognition she would get from volunteering her services. Constantly encouraging us to do better and believe in the good and right thing, Emily Schroeder is a woman of true virtue. I genuinely and honestly thank her and CASA for such a positive and constructive experience in my life.

I began to comprehend what was available to me as a youth in foster care, including money for college. At this time, I am very proud of myself and my many accomplishments, including an induction into the National Honor Role 2003–2004, my role as President of the Lexington Chapter I Business Professionals of America, my acceptance into Texas A&M University—Commerce, and being a member of CASEY Youth Panel.

I am very dedicated to advocating for foster youth in the system, as well as trying to find ways to help better the national foster care system. I am currently the head member of the Texas Preparation for Adult Living (PAL) Youth Leadership Committee, and I represent my region at the state level. As a member of the committee, I work very closely with other members to better the Texas foster care system. The committee is currently working on the *Texas Foster Care Handbook*, which provides everything we feel foster youth should know about the foster care system, including chain of command, names or labels that may arise, explanation of commonly used phrases or words, an in-depth clarification of the PAL benefits, personal anecdotes, quotes from the leadership committee members, and other interesting information. It also provides answers to questions that might arise while a youth is residing in the foster care system. We feel that foster youth have rights and every youth should know about all of the things afforded to him or her as a youth in foster care.

Now, as I look towards the future, I can reflect back on the days of my past and laugh with my family, friends, and loved ones. I can talk about how I was raised and how my life began with an early introduc-

tion to the fast lane. I can do all of this reflecting with ease and enjoyment. I thank everyone who has helped me on this long journey to success—my foster family, CPS caseworker, placement agency, PAL affiliates, and CASA. I pray that God continue to bless and guide each and every one of these gracious individuals. These were my CASA experiences. I hope they inspire a positive future for foster youth. Once again, thank you.

Motivation and Inspiration

By Pam Byrd

Until this day, I can remember Emily coming into our room with a great big smile, encouraging us to be successful.

Having a CASA worker is like having a best friend who you can trust in the time of pain and distress.

My CASA worker, Emily Schroeder, was there for my brother and me when no one else was. Emily was there when we fought our biggest struggles in foster care. She inspired us both when we felt most uninspired.

Throughout our experience in foster care, Emily motivated my brother and me in every aspect of being successful. She motivated us both to keep our grades up and stay in school. She also motivated us to dig deep within to overcome our toughest emotions.

When my brother and I first met our CASA worker, Emily Schroeder, we were at our first foster home in Lexington, Texas. We received a message that someone was there to see us. We both though that it was someone coming to tell us more bad news. This put more stress on us both. Until this day, I can remember Emily coming into our room with a great big smile, encouraging us to be successful. This gave us a high level of confidence. From that day on, my brother and I overcame our challenges and achieved

many things. We are both currently making all As and Bs and are exempt from all of our semester exams, and we are in a much lower level of care.

Frequently, Emily puts her personal life on hold to see that the needs of her CASA children are met.

Reaching out to other foster care youth is one of my greatest concerns, especially those who do not have a CASA worker. My CASA worker helped me get into activities and take leadership roles. I am an annual participant in PAL Camp Independence. My CASA worker introduced this to me.

I also participated in the 2003 PEAKS Adventure Camp, which allowed me to make some discoveries about myself. Throughout this camp, I demonstrated my strengths and the power I have within. Emily's motivations and her encouragements helped my brother Lerrion become very active in the Youth Leadership Committee conferences. He is also a peer leader participant in the PEAKS adventure camp. There he motivates and encourages others. He is also the youth representative for foster youth in our region. He flies in and out of the state to better the Texas foster care system and improve youths' rights, visitation rights, the chain of command in case of a problem, PAL activities, PAL benefits, and implementing the recommendations made at the Texas Teen conference. My brother, Lerrion, stands strong as a voice for youth in foster care. The summit of what I am trying to say is that Emily inspired my brother to be active and successful. Through his achievements, my brother inspired me to stand up and take pride in being in foster care. Now, I want to take the role of my older brother and be an inspiration to someone else.

I am currently running for the PAL Youth Leadership Committee representative for my region so I can be a voice for those who are in the foster care system. In additional to this, I enrolled to take part in the 2003 Texas Teen Conference.

Emily knew my focus was acting. She went out of her way to see that I have the opportunity to become an actor. Emily asked some of the generous people at her job to donate the money for acting lessons.

As you can see, Emily put forth so much effort to ensure our success, and without Emily's immense inspiration and concern, I would not have the motivation or the desire to make a difference in the lives of others. ←

Terrill Evans
Morganton, North Carolina
North Carolina Guardian ad Litem Program, Judicial District 3B

"The system let him down," guardian ad litem volunteer Iris Derrick says of 19-year-old Terrill Evans. In some states, like North Carolina, CASA volunteers are referred to as guardian ad litems. He had been in the foster care system for a number of years, but, in his early teens, Terrill was placed back with his mother on a trial basis. Iris felt it was a setting where he lacked sufficient supervision and guidance. She was advocating for Terrill to enter a strong group home program when the 14-year-old was involved in a crime in his neighborhood.

When Terrill's case entered the juvenile justice system, the Division of Social Services wanted to close his file. Iris fought to keep Terrill's case active with DSS so the unit would help Terrill's mother with visitation if she desired it and would still provide some financial support for him. Her insistence, along with a supportive judge, kept Terrill's case active until he was 18.

Iris says that although incarceration is never a good thing, Terrill has made it as positive as possible. He worked to earn his general equivalency diploma (GED) shortly after entering the facility and is staying focused on his goals. She says the corrections personnel marvel at Terrill's skills on the basketball court and say he has become a great role model for other youth in the facility. Iris stays in touch with him through cards and letters.

Terrill will be about 25 when he is released from detention, and Iris says that although he'll be playing catch-up for a while, he has the potential and intelligence to be a strong member of the community.

It's All Up to Me Now

So while I'm incarcerated I will seize any opportunity to achieve my dream.
Like my guardian told me, it's all up to me now.

The guardian ad litem is a great program for kids who feel they are alone and unwanted. That was how I felt when I was in foster care. My guardian always encouraged me to give my best at whatever I do. She always told me I have a lot of potential, but I focus it towards negative things. It took incarceration for me to grasp that concept.

From the moment I was in custody, I started thinking about my education. I applied myself and received my GED within four months through a community college in the area.

At the place of my incarceration, I found a lot of kids like me who felt alone and unwanted so I reached out to them and told them that they were in a similar situation as I was. I offered my advice to them using what my guardian told me and a little more. I told them to give their best to what they do, and always remember that someone is there if you need them. Also, never let go of dreams because the sky is the limit. I want to play professional basketball or own a barbershop when I'm released. So while I'm incarcerated, I will seize any opportunity to achieve my dream. Like my guardian told me, it's all up to me now. Even though I am no longer in the program, my guardian keeps in touch to see if I'm still doing okay, and I'm very grateful. Overall, the guardian ad litem program is excellent for children who need encouragement and guidance outside of a regular foster home.

Anthony Gill
Austin, Texas
Travis County CASA

Anthony "Jerome" Gill was a kid who wanted to believe in superheroes, to think it possible that some mighty character could right the world for him. It turned out that a hero did come, just in the slightly more modest form of an architect and CASA volunteer.

Volunteer Karen Cox doesn't have any exceptional powers, she just recognized Jerome as a smart, funny, sensitive young man with great potential. The two spent time together and talked easily, and, even after Jerome found a secure, long-term foster care placement, Karen kept tabs on his case. "Somebody just needed to be watching out for him," she says of that time.

Karen tried to teach Jerome the small things in life—how to open a door for a woman, how to order and handle the check in a restaurant. But she also saw him through tough moments, like saying good-bye to his baby sister when she was adopted and settling into his foster home when he decided he didn't want to be considered for adoption.

Karen says Jerome was clearly quite brilliant, but was often too busy making his classmates laugh to pay attention to the teacher. "It was a challenge for him to stay focused through school," Karen says. But Jerome graduated and is now in his second year of college. He's studying film, photography, and drama, and wants to make movies.

Jerome says he calls Karen "Wonder Woman" in his essay because it describes how strong she really is. "It takes someone dedicated to get involved in kids' lives not only when they're doing well but when they're doing badly," Jerome says. Karen is no longer serving as a CASA volunteer to Jerome and his siblings, but that hasn't ended their relationship. They talk almost every week. "We're like family," Jerome says.

Wonder Woman

Whenever you say CASA, you do not say, "Here is my well-paid CASA worker." Nope, not at all.
Whenever you mention CASA, you say, "Here is my CASA volunteer."

Hello everyone. My name is Anthony Davidson Gill, although I go by Jerome Gill because that is the name my mother has called me since I was born. I am going to tell you what it is like to have a CASA volunteer. First off, just notice the title. Whenever you say CASA, you do not say, "Here is my well-paid CASA worker." Nope, not at all. Whenever you mention CASA, you say, "Here is my CASA volunteer." That means you have someone caring and loving you for you, not the state's or the government's money.

My mom shook our baby sister, which led to me, my two little sisters, and our older brother being placed into foster care. As time went by, my mother told CPS that she could not take care of us. We traveled from being in a shelter to being put into our first foster home. This is where I would meet, Karen Cox, a special lady who I call Wonder Woman.

I remember the time when my CASA worker and I first went in court, and I was oh so very nervous. I thought, here comes another state worker telling me what to do. So I was not happy at first. Then she came to visit me when I was 12 years of age. Karen and I talked, and once she took my siblings and me out to get ice cream.

There was also a time when I had to say good-bye to my little sister, and that was so hard for me to handle. She was adopted by someone I didn't know. All I knew and felt was that my baby sister was being taken away. I did not have my mom telling me, "everything will be fine." I did not have Superman to cheer me. There was no Captain Planet there to clean up my tears. I had no hero except my CASA worker. She was there. Not my mom, not my dad, and I guess Superman just forgot to show up. I had no Superman, but I did, and still do have a Wonder Woman. My CASA worker was strong enough for me that day to overpower 100 Supermen. She was there taking pictures, laughing, and having fun with us. I was dead inside, and she was my respirator keeping me alive. The following week, Karen brought my siblings and me pictures of our good-bye visit with our little sister. I was so happy with what she had done.

I am now 19 years old and in college. I graduated from Lockhart High School, and, of course, Wonder Woman was there and brought my younger sister (not the adopted one). I am very thankful to CASA, so thankful that I had to return the favor. For CASA, I put my life out there to everyone. I have been to two interviews on Fox 7 and one for Channel 8. I have told Fox 7 my life. I have told news reporters how much I love my CASA and the things she has done for me. I was so scared to tell my story at first, then I realized I have already lived through this. I am still alive, and handsome, so let's do this.

I will be the first to admit I'm not perfect, but I have given Karen permission to use my life story to inspire other kids in similar situations. I am so lucky to have a CASA volunteer that I can call Aunt Karen, and to hear her say she loves me and call me "son." She was so happy the time I got to speak at the Texas Mansion for a CASA fundraiser. I got a haircut, and CASA raised so much money. I can't even sum it all up with only a thousand words, but I can sum it up in three very simple words, I love her. She was always there for my family and me, and she still is.

Teairrow Hill
Dallas, Texas
Dallas CASA, Inc.

CASA volunteer Rebecca Rios says 13-year-old Teairrow Hill was one tough young woman when they first met. With her shoulders squared to any newcomer, she was streetwise, stoic, and suspicious. "She had learned to put up a tough front," Rebecca says. Teairrow was, however, willing to let Rebecca in enough to see if she could get her what she most wanted—the chance to see her younger siblings. The family had been in the system about a year and a half, and the five children wound up in placements all over the county.

Rebecca worked to arrange the visit and says that watching the teen with her brothers and sister is how she got to know the real Teairrow. "During the sibling visits, she would become loving, caring, and compassionate," says Rebecca. "Her way of speaking changed and you realized how educated she was."

Rebecca says she still had to work with Teairrow on all the anger she had stored up inside. She was dealing with so much hurt and pain that small things would set her off. "Her behavior would just become so explosive," Rebecca says. So she started encouraging her to write every night. It was a way to allow Teairrow to get her feelings and anger and frustration out and have some time to reflect and de-escalate. "She can count on getting a diary from me each year," Rebecca says.

Several years ago, Teairrow was recognized as one of the highest achievers in the district in English. Most of the winners had crowds of people there. Teairrow just had Rebecca to cheer her accomplishment. But the award and getting recognized in writing contests have helped Teairrow realize that academics can be important and rewarding. Rebecca says the now 16-year-old has become calmer and more confident. She has also found she loves working with young children, and Rebecca says she is terrific with them.

In the Eyes of a Foster Child

She asked me if there was something I truly wanted. I replied yes.
I wanted to see my brothers and my sister. The next weekend, I was having a visit.

I never knew this would happen to me. At age 11, my four younger siblings and I were separated from my grandmother. A year later, I was told I could never go home. Child Protective Services cut off all of my visits. Then, months later, a woman from CASA, Rebecca Rios, came to visit me. She asked me if there was something I truly wanted. I replied yes. I wanted to see my brothers and my sister. The next weekend, I was having a visit. After that I knew she would be with me forever. I considered her my caseworker because she worked on my case more than any caseworker had. Mrs. Rios was my inspiration to write. She showed me ways to let go of anger. At that time, writing was one of them. She inspired me to do other unique things that would let out my feelings. I was a very angry child. I could get mad at her for stupid things, and she still showed me love. When I had questions, I could count on her to answer them. She has also been there for me to talk to her. She is more to me than what her job asks of her. She is my friend, a mentor, and my comforter.

I am now 15 years old, and in my years as a foster child, I have given them nothing but trouble. I didn't like to listen; always wanted to fight. I am now trying to start over before it is too late. I have learned that if I don't make a change now, it will be hard for me when I become an adult. Some of the things people tell me I used to do make me laugh and say, "I used to be BAD." I tell a lot of younger kids in care that the things adults tell you will benefit you later in life. You may believe they are wrong, but you still have to do what they tell you to do. I can remember when I used to take all the bad things that happened as an excuse to act up. I now know that if I rob a bank, I can't say I was brought up to do that.

I love little kids, so now I spend my time helping my foster parents. I teach the little ones about their hygiene, even the older ones. I try to show them to take their problems and make the best of them. I help my foster parents clean and cook so that they may have a break. One of my foster brothers is having trouble learning, so I help him with his homework. I learned you will one day repent for your bad doings. I use my pain and struggles as a testimony to what God has done for me. I want to be a successful person. I decided to make a difference in my life so that I may help others. ✦

Michelle Ann Holbrook
Escondido, California
Voices for Children Inc.

Susan Walton was a new CASA volunteer when she got Michelle Holbrook's case. Then 15, Michelle was in group home with strict rules, and Susan was one of the few people who could expose her to some of her strengths. Michelle found one of those strengths on the day Susan took her to see a presentation by the Real Word panel at Voices for Children. The Real Word is a group of teens formerly or currently in foster care who talk to their peers and community groups about life in the foster care system. Susan says Michelle watched intently as the young people on the panel gave presentations and answered questions. During the panel, Michelle turned to Susan and said, "I could never do that." But as the presentation continued, and Michelle thought more about it, she changed her tune. "You know what, I think I could do that," Susan remembers her saying. And she could.

Sabrina Goosby, who oversees the Real Word for Voices for Children, says Michelle is great on the panel and is especially good at answering questions from other teens on how to handle their anger, frustrations, and impatience—something Michelle has had to work through herself. "Michelle pushes the envelope," says Sabrina. "She asks questions and wants to know why. Why is the rule that way?" Sabrina also says Michelle is a perfectionist who wants to get things right and get them done right away. In some situations, these qualities have served the bright, red-headed teen well. With Susan's advocacy and support, Michelle was able to get into a better academic program, catch up in school, and graduate with all As. Those same qualities, however, can also be tough on those around her. "Her other panel members will tell her to chill out sometimes," Sabrina says.

Michelle has learned to pour her energy into writing, soccer, music, dancing, basketball, and collecting 46 pairs of shoes. She is looking forward to beginning college, moving into her first apartment, and getting started on her career goals. With her energy and intensity, there's no doubt she'll reach them all.

Finding My Voice

Susan Walton was the only adult in my life brave enough, courageous enough, kind, loving, and honest enough to be there for me.

I am a graduating senior at San Pasqual Academy with a 3.8 GPA. I have resided in the foster care system for seven years. For two of those years, I was blessed with a phenomenal CASA worker named Susan Walton.

I was still getting into a heck of a lot of trouble when Miss Walton came into my life. I had left my group home without permission more than 15 times, and I was sexually active and drinking. I don't know how or why, but I feel her presence gave me back the security that was ripped from my foundation at such a young age. I was 14 years old when Susan was assigned to me as her first case. I was in my 24th school, 11th placement, and at the low point of a deeply troubled relationship with my county worker. She was my angel in my time of need. More specifically, Susan Walton was deeply connected into every aspect of my life, including my education plan meetings, court dates, family visitations, and extracurricular activities. She was a friend who helped me improve my study and organizational skills, guided me through scholarship applications, and helped me resolve conflicts with people in my life. She helped me realize my county worker's abuse by showing me her love and support. She cared and she listened. My county worker wouldn't let me play sports, go to school functions, work, move to a less restrictive placement, or speak to friends without supervision. Susan helped me write several people in the system about my feelings.

This was done because Susan Walton was the only adult in my life brave enough, courageous enough, kind, loving, and honest enough to be there for me. No other adult has proven such commitment as Susan Walton has to me. Susan also realized the importance of a good education. I had never been allowed to enroll in a public school before she took my case. She noticed the effect on my learning and took the needed steps to get me the quality of education I needed. By working hard in an independent study program, I passed my freshman, sophomore, and junior years in one year and graduated on time.

As many of you may know, foster youth do not have a voice in the system that is powerful like that of an adult. Susan made me see that I too could have powerful voice when she introduced me to the Real Word teen speaker's bureau for Voices for Children. I found the answer for all my built-up stress and my need to let other people in the community know of the life for foster youth. My voice became a voice that mattered. I have been a part of this panel for about two years now and it is my number one love. This is how I give back to youth who are not spoken for. I speak for them and for their fearful hearts. I speak to large groups of CASA volunteers, social workers, staff, attorneys, child workers, and foster parents. I speak to anyone interested. I have also applied to be a youth mentor at the Employment Development Department as a youth assistant. I would be helping youth stay in school and placing them into jobs that match their interests. Furthermore, I help youth in need by offering tutoring at the San Pasqual Academy during homework hours. I am very dedicated to my using my life as a foster youth to better the foster care system.

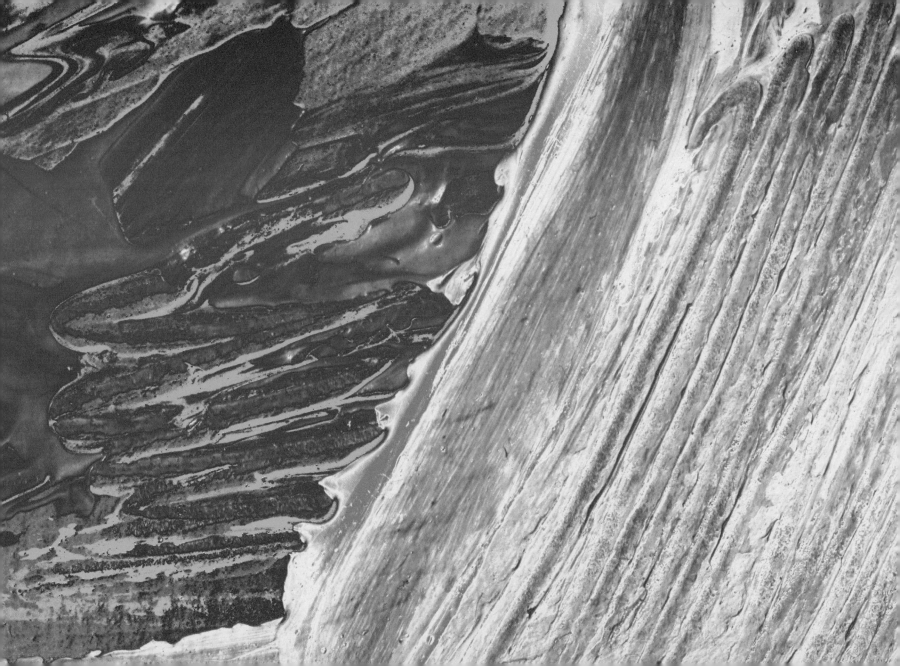

Norma and Juan Holguin
Loveland, Colorado
CASA Inc. of Larimer County

The young lives of Norma and Juan Holguin have been far from charmed, but the two kind, talented teens were given a new beginning that could be described as nearly storybook.

Carol Alford, a longtime CASA volunteer, writer and retired school teacher, stepped into the siblings' lives when they were removed from their mother's home. Carol felt she could help the children by taking them on short outings that gave her an opportunity to become better acquainted and build trust with the two children. She says the three of them also had a great time together.

Carol was also a fierce advocate for Juan and Norma. When the apartment they were living in with their older sister, Michelle, was damaged, Carol helped find emergency funds. And when Michelle—just out of her teens herself—found that caring for her two siblings was more than she could handle, Carol helped stabilize Juan and Norma's placement and found them the supplies and clothes they needed to go back to school.

Both teens have powerful spirits, good hearts, and positive attitudes that have served them well, according to Carol. She says Juan decided to volunteer in the school cafeteria to help "cover" his free lunch program, and when he couldn't pay for a school field trip, the cafeteria workers collected the money for him to go. And Norma, in addition to playing several sports and participating in orchestra and clubs, translates for other parents and students in her school. It was the parents of one of Norma's friends from her many activities who heard about Norma and Juan's situation and opened their home. The couple had three high schoolers already and had also taken in a young niece and nephew. Norma and Juan made seven kids in their bustling but ordered household.

Carol says the family has created a setting where everyone helps out, everyone is an equal part of the family, and everyone feels welcome and loved. Norma and Juan clearly feel that they have found a home.

As I Felt Loved

By Norma Holguin

As you can see, Juan and I have a second chance to live a better life with this wonderful family. Through the qualities that they have shown us, we are learning to live life with smiles and laughs and we have a chance to be a kid and teen again.

I know I made the right choice
By looking in their eyes
They seem happy
As they have accepted us into their lives
They bring us joy
Happiness and support
That I never felt before
I see their smiles
Shining on their face
I see my life in a better place
When they talk to me
I feel that they care
Our cultures may be a little different
But their support will always be there
As I feel love
Deep inside me
I begin to leave what's behind me
As we are living together
I feel the presence of a family
That I never experienced before
I thank the Lord every day
For the guardian angels He has sent
To me
I'm thankful for them to choose me.

My poem presents how a family should be, the family that every child dreams of. But some of us are not lucky enough to have one like this. This is my way of showing my new family my love and appreciation.

How did I find this home and family? It all began when my parents came from Mexico to the United States searching for work. Eventually all five of us kids joined them. It wasn't easy. As life went on, the family didn't stay together. Three of my siblings dropped out of school to get jobs, but my brother and I were determined to get an education. We were dreaming that we were going to become firefighters, doctors, teachers, coaches, and even the President of the United States when we grew up.

I am growing up. I am on my way to the future. One of the reasons I feel so confident is because of my new family, the Cohoons.

Because of my mother's abusive behavior, the court removed my brother and me from her custody. For a while we were living with my sister Michelle, who was 23 at the time. Finally, she couldn't handle the responsibility of two teens. We were left homeless at Christmas time. It was the worst Christmas I ever had. I worried about losing my education, friends, coaches, and my teachers. I was afraid of losing the opportunity to become a U.S. citizen and the possibility of losing scholarships that could take me to a higher place in life. At this, the Cohoons came to my rescue. Their daughters, Laura and Natasha, were involved in sports with me at Mountain View High School, and Laura was in orchestra with me. On New Year's Day, the Cohoons decided that my brother and I could stay with them.

I am grateful that the courts designated the Cohoons as my kinship family and we now have a stable and secure home. Even though we come from a different culture and a different background, we have a chance to live in a family that doesn't yell when we do something right—like homework; doesn't hit us with different objects; doesn't make us feel like we are in jail; doesn't tell us that we are dumb or stupid. Now we have a family that is supportive and understanding; that cares, loves, and respects every person; and has open communication.

As you can see, Juan and I have a second chance to live a better life with this wonderful family. Through the qualities that they have shown us, we are learning to live life with smiles and laughs and we have a chance to be a kid and teen again.

Though I did not trust the system or the courts and social services in the beginning, a good thing happened. We met Carol Alford. She is the CASA volunteer who is our mentor and friend. She helped us get school supplies for the year because she knew that school was important to us. She also helped my sister get help when her apartment was flooded.

She is one of the people from the courts and social services who hasn't left us behind. CASA is a very good program because they care about people like us and the way we are treated.

When we were young and in our early teens, we had a hard life without parents to support and guide us. I had to accomplish everything on my own and also be a role model for my little brother Juan. You would think with my background I would end up doing drugs, using alcohol, or committing suicide. But no, I'm involved in many activities, including tutoring, track, soccer, softball, basketball, swimming, flag team, orchestra, peer counseling, and LULAC (the League of United Latin American Citizens).

I have many goals for the future, but my immediate ones are to make a difference in the lives of my new family members. I love helping out with the two youngest who are 5 and 8. As a family we watch movies and go to church, picnics, and family gatherings. I do my part with chores, cooking meals, and planning special activities. Awesome life!!

Unconditional Love

By Juan Holguin

"You have grown out of your seashell," said Miss Berry, my PE teacher.
Yes, I have, because I now open my heart even more to show my love.

I was just a babe. I had much to learn. I had much to understand. My eyes looked up into this new world, this new country.

Although my homeland was Mexico, it would never be a home to me again. My parents found work in this new country and struggled to support five children. In those years, I did not imagine that my family would become a troubled family.

I don't remember my father because he returned to Mexico long ago. As time went on, I saw my mother change completely. She was difficult to live with, and I could never understand what she was saying or what she expected of me. Usually, she made me feel unimportant, never went to any of my activities, and made me feel stupid. We weren't allowed to have friends over. I sometimes miss my mom. Sometime I don't. I just wish she could have been there when I needed her the most. I felt like it was a mistake for me to live. The only supportive people were my school teachers, friends, and staff workers.

When I was a seventh grader, the courts took custody of my older sister and me. We were afraid of being separated from our family and went to live with our sister Michelle, who was 23 years old at that time. We tried to make things work, but it was too much responsibility for her. Michelle asked us to leave, and she moved to another state. It was Christmas, and I was homeless.

A wonderful family heard about our problems and accepted us into their home. Since it was temporary, at first I was scared about the future. Where will I live next? What is going to happen?

Things went well. We had found a family who loved us. We felt secure and now, through the kinship program, the Cohoons are generally recognized as my "parents."

When the court removed me from my mother's home, I was fortunate to find a new friend. She is my CASA friend, Carol. Carol has been so great to me since we met. She has supported me with help buying school supplies and clothes. Carol helped my sister Michelle by gathering some money for a place to live when we had to move because of rain damage. Carol keeps in contact with us through the days. When we have a question for the caseworker and we can't get a hold of her, she tries to communicate with her as well. The most important thing of all is that she liked to have fun.

We are a family of nine. The amazing thing about the coming fall is that five of use will be attending the same high school. We will have one freshman, one sophomore, one junior, and two seniors. We will be involved in many different activities. What is also amazing is that we will have a high school graduate every year.

I would not call this a "foster home." I would call this a home where I'm welcome to live. As for my appreciation, I help take care of their nephews who live with us. We have so much fun together that many people think I'm their big brother. Often I do feel like their big brother. I cannot explain what the feeling is like, because it is the most incredible feeling ever. I'm even inspired to keep their house clean and tidy.

This family has done so much for me that my life has changed completely. Some of the things they have brought into my life are good communication, an appreciation for who I am, happiness when I'm feeling low, a feeling of being at home, and encouragement in the things I do. Being in their home makes me feel warm inside and there is always a smile to greet me when I come home from school.

Because of my CASA friend and my kinship parents, I am confident about my future. Already, I have improved on communication with others, and I'm not so quiet anymore. I used to not laugh a lot, but now they fill my heart with love. They also help me prepare for my future. With their help, I will soon be able to get my U.S. citizenship.

I've always felt like an American, but I will then legally be an American.

My dream that I had since I was a little kid was being a bilingual teacher. Now I think that dream is possible. I've seen many teachers having fun and enjoying their jobs. I love helping students in class when they don't understand something. During my school years, I translate for those Spanish speaking students and parents who do not know how to speak English.

"You have grown out of your seashell," said Miss Berry, my PE teacher. Yes, I have, because I now open my heart even more to show my love. What has happened to me over these tiring, hard, and struggling years shall never be forgotten. As for my mother, I want to tell her that my future looks great.

Tabitha Joplin
Claremore, Oklahoma
Tri-County CASA

Tabitha Joplin was too young to remember Virginia Huey when she was serving as her CASA volunteer. She says she has some memories of being in the courtroom, but has no images of the woman who was battling for her safety and well-being there. As Tabitha became old enough to understand, however, her adoptive parents told her about how they turned to CASA when they feared that sending Tabitha to live with her paternal grandparents wasn't the best thing for this traumatized baby who cried all the time. The caseworkers and judges felt it was hard to turn away from relatives, especially relatives who wanted the little girl.

Tabitha's three older brothers had already been removed from home and placed with the grandparents. To see for herself what kind of home the grandparents could provide and what kind of support and counseling Tabitha would get there, Virginia, a single mom of four, drove to a rural town in Texas and started knocking on doors, talking to teachers, and visiting with family. She wasn't encouraged by what she found.

Virginia's work led to a meeting with the grandparents, Tabitha, and the Joplins, Tabitha's foster parents at the time. Virginia says the grandparents were willing to let Tabitha stay put after observing her with the Joplins.

Even after Virginia moved to Houston, she kept in touch with Tabitha through letters and a few visits over the years. "She knows I like to read and she sends me books," Tabitha says of Virginia. The 15-year-old high school sophomore likes to play soccer, write stories, and sing. She asked to enter a talent show several years ago and won first prize for her performance of "My Heart Will Go On."

Tabitha may not remember Virginia when she was advocating for her, but she has been grateful for her involvement every day since.

A Life Saved

I was assigned a CASA worker, and she promised to be at the hearing the next day.
I know her willingness to change her schedule to attend a hearing
really did save my life.

I had been living in the homeless shelter in downtown Tulsa, Oklahoma, for a long time when, at the age of 14 months, I stumbled into the loving arms of two very caring individuals. While I was living in the shelter, a social worker telephoned a woman with graying hair who was in her forties. The social worker asked her if she would accept another foster child. She said that she wouldn't mind, so they brought me out to the gingerbread brick house that afternoon, and I met my new family.

Not long after that, a knowledgeable doctor diagnosed me with attachment disorder. I wouldn't eat. I wouldn't sleep. I cried all night. It was as though I was testing—testing to see if they would still love me if I wasn't the perfect child at 17 months of age.

One day the social worker called my foster mother and said that I would probably be returned to my birthrelatives the next day. She asked her to have my things packed and ready to go. My foster mom and dad were convinced that somehow they had to save me. I came from a home with possible abuse and much neglect from my schizophrenic mother and drug-abusive father. So when my foster mother called the social worker, she suggested that we contact CASA.

The director of the CASA program was familiar with my case, even though this was my first time in foster care. I was assigned a CASA worker, and she promised to be at the hearing the next day. I know that her willingness to change her schedule to attend a hearing really did save my life. CASA's intervention kept me from being returned to a dangerous situation.

During the next two and a half years, the CASA volunteer visited extensively with everyone involved in my case—my birthparents, foster parents, and family members. She was at every hearing and even went out of state to interview family members that wanted me placed with them. She visited the school where these family members had sent my older siblings and she read every word of my psychological evaluation. She took the time to do this even though she was a full-time parent with teenagers and a full-time job. A big thank you goes out to her employer who was very accommodating and let her have time off to attend the court hearings!

The Department of Human Services still pursued sending me to blood relatives. These relatives had my older siblings, but they had failed to get counseling for them and had decided on their own that my siblings didn't need counseling—they didn't need a professional's advice.

At the hearing, the social worker had to follow her supervisor's instructions, even though she did not agree. But my CASA volunteer spoke her mind and, by doing so, caused the judge to question the social worker and allowed her to state her opinion, not just her supervisor's opinion. If it were not for the tenacity of the CASA, this case, my life, would have had a drastically different outcome. The CASA volunteer didn't have to consider anything except what was best for me.

When I was 3 years old, much to my foster parents' surprise, they were asked if they would be interested in adopting me. They knew they were over the age limit, but the quickly agreed with a resounding YES. We were a legal family soon after. Because of the love and caring of my CASA worker, I was released from considering myself simply "a foster child." I was now a daughter, legal and legitimate. No one could ever again tell my parents that I wasn't their daughter. I continued to get the counseling I needed. When I was 5 years old, I was diagnosed with attention deficit disorder, and, at 8 years of age, I was diagnosed with Tourette's.

I am now 15 years old and attend a local Christian school where I will be entering the 10th grade in the fall. I enjoy most of my studies, play soccer, and relax with my friends. My soccer team won the state championship last year. I enjoy working with middle and upper elementary children, and will be helping to teach Vacation Bible School at my church this summer for the third year. Also, I have pursued singing for the last six years of my life, and enjoy drama and theater. I recently made a CD at the Greenwood Studios in Tulsa entitled "Tabitha Ann, Live from Big Oaks."

I have had the advantage of counseling and great doctors that have helped me with my attachment disorder, ADD, and Tourette's. And, most of all, I have a great mom and dad. All of this would not have been possible without the help of my CASA volunteer. She saved my life.

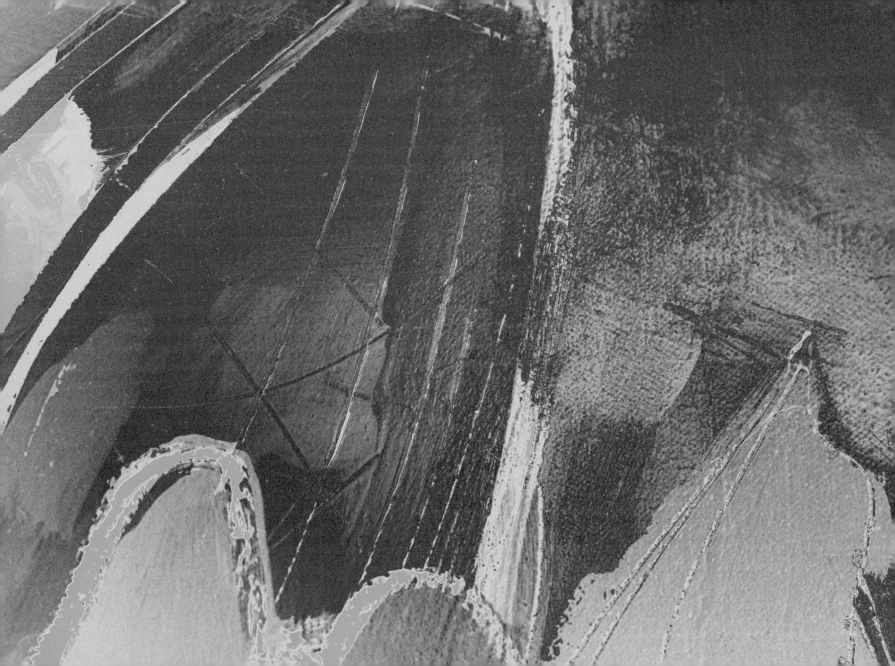

Kimberly Lundy
Angie, Louisiana
Youth Services Bureau CASA Program

In the eight years CASA volunteer Barbara Ponson has known 19-year-old Kimberly Lundy, their relationship has had some ups and downs. When Barbara first got Kimberly's case, the 12-year-old was standoffish and skeptical of this new person in her life. Barbara says Kim would just watch coolly as she played with and talked to her younger sister. After a while, Kimberly warmed up to Barbara, and she was able to be a friend and an advocate for her.

As Kim went through two pregnancies in her teens, Barbara was willing to become the bad guy again when Kim wanted to drop out of school. "No, that's not an option," Barbara told her. She says she backed off of the tender loving care and pushed hard for Kim to see high school through to graduation. "There were three or four years with Kim that I wasn't her favorite person," says Barbara. "I would call and ask, 'Are you still mad at me?' and get nothing but an 'Uh huh' from the other line."

But Kim stayed in school, and not only graduated but graduated near the top of her class. On the day Kim learned that she had earned the ACT score she needed to qualify for Louisiana's Tuition Opportunity Program for Students, which pays tuition and fees to state universities, her principal let her call Barbara from school. Barbara says Kim was in a state of happy hysteria on the phone.

Kim now lives with her two children and their father in a tiny campus apartment. She is in her second year of school and has happy, healthy kids according to Barbara. "I think I had a part in Kim's success, but I had a lot to work with," Barbara says. "She is very bright and had a desire to succeed."

Louisiana's CASA program, however, thinks Barbara must have a lot to do with the success of the many young people she has served. She was recognized as CASA Volunteer of the Year in her region and then for the entire state. She says CASA has just become part of who she is.

Kim was thrilled to hear Barbara had gotten recognized for her CASA work, and wishes there was more she could do to thank her for the role she played in her life; "There is so much I wish I could do to show her my appreciation."

CASA: A Volunteer to Love

If I didn't have a volunteer there to push me to do my best,
I probably would not be where I am today.

Life can be very hard when you are placed in foster care. Foster children sometimes feel lonely and depressed when placed in a home with complete strangers. Even though I had foster parents, I needed someone else there to help me get through those lonesome and miserable days. That's where a CASA volunteer steps in and lends you a hand in filling those dark spots.

A CASA volunteer is always there to help you make it through those tough times in foster care. You don't have many people willing to volunteer their time to help hard-headed foster kids. My CASA is always trying her very best to help me. I know that she volunteered because she cared. I appreciate her for all her dedication and time, because she didn't have to volunteer to help me. She pushed me to strive for the best, and she always reminded me that to have the best I have to be the best. I have taken those words to heart. Whenever I feel that I want to give up, those words always come back and remind me to keep striving to be the best. I am happy I had the opportunity to have a CASA.

My CASA wasn't just a volunteer there to make sure I received everything I needed; she also became my best friend. Assigning me a CASA was one of the best things the state could have done for me. If I didn't have a volunteer there to push me to do my best, I probably would not be where I am today. She became my second mom and mentor; someone I trusted to guide me through life. Being in foster care was hard; kids teased me at school and I felt left out. I needed someone to talk to, someone who understood how I was feeling. My CASA helped me to look beyond those obstacles and focus on the good things in life. She has always been there to help me. I had wonderful foster parents, but sometimes there were certain things that I didn't want to talk to them about. When I couldn't talk to them I could always call Mrs. Barbara. Sometimes I had nightmares and felt depressed, but no matter what time of the night I could always call her to talk about my problems.

I had two children while I was in foster care, and she was always there to help me cope with the challenges of being a young mother. She was there when both of my kids were born and for their birthday parties.

When I was pregnant with my second child, I wanted to drop out of high school and take care of my children. Mrs. Barbara sat me down and told me that she understood what I was going through and that life isn't easy, but my life would be what I made of it. She told me she wasn't mad, but being a dropout wasn't trying to be the best. I knew that I didn't want to work at McDonald's all my life so I decided to finish school.

Teachers said I wasn't going to make it because I had two kids and was taking Algebra II and advanced math to graduate with honors. Mrs. Barbara taught me to take negative comments and turn them into incentives to achieve my goals. That is what I did. Mrs. Barbara was there when I graduated from high school with honors and a 3.5 GPA. I was number five in my class and the only African American in my graduating class to receive a scholarship through the Tuition Opportunity Program for Students. She helped me to apply for admission to Louisiana State University and find more financial support. She pushed me to do my best because she knew what I was capable of and wanted to see me succeed.

Even though I am out of foster care, I can still call her to help me with certain problems. During my first semester at LSU, I wasn't doing well, and I wasn't used to getting bad grades on tests. I remember calling her and crying about my grades. She told me her daughter went through the same thing during her freshman year at LSU. She told me she knew I could make it through that first semester, and, when I did, my second semester would be smooth sailing. She has never guided me wrong, and just as she said my second semester was very easy. I don't know how others feel or felt about their volunteers, but I love mine. If I had a million dollars it wouldn't be enough to repay her for what she had done for me. I don't have a million dollars, but I do appreciate and cherish everything she's done.

I have a little sister in foster care and she is going through some of the things I went through. I try to help her cope with her problems. I find myself at times sounding like my CASA when I am talking to her. I try to push her to be the best. I want to be there for her because someone was there for me. I want her to be able to look up to me for anything and know that her big sister will always be there no matter what. I'm always teaching her what I have learned because I want her to do her best. If there were a CASA volunteer for every child in the world, I believe the world would be a better place.

Cherline Norvilus
Port Charlotte, Florida
Lee County Guardian ad Litem

When Carol Alver, a longtime guardian ad litem, went to meet 14-year-old Cherline Norvilus for the first time, she brought along a few books, hoping the two could connect through them. When they started talking, Carol asked Cherline what she liked to read. "Shakespeare," was Cherline's answer. Carol figured that she and this bright young woman would get along just fine.

Cherline found another lover of words when she was put in a placement in Charlotte County, Florida. Bev McFerren, a retired school teacher who used to teach young people to write poetry, filled in as Cherline's guardian while she was too far from Carol to see her regularly. Cherline and Bev used poetry as a way to communicate and get to know one another. Bev says when she read Cherline's poem, "Why Do I Cry," it hit her so hard she felt the need to respond. Poetry seemed the natural way to answer the pained questions Cherline poses in her piece.

Cherline says she started writing after reading a book of poetry. "I felt what it was saying to me, so I started to write my own on my life." And it was a remarkable and painful young life she had to record. Born in Haiti, Cherline's father was killed when she was 7 years old, and her aunt brought her over to America. "All I remember was that I was on a plane and was looking at the blue, beautiful sky," Cherline writes about the experience. "After flying for hours, I entered a whole new place.

A place I've never seen before. The grass was so green. I saw stop signs and all different races of people together."

Her aunt left her with some family friends who Cherline says abused her and turned her into a household servant. The one bright spot during this time was a second-grade teacher who taught Cherline some English and encouraged her to read and study. At 14, Cherline ran away from home and wound up in a series of foster care placements. Now 16, she is in a strong foster home, and Carol hopes it will give her a chance to get more consistent services and counseling. As her advocate, Carol has been battling with immigration services for several years to get the documents Cherline needs to become a legal resident. She says Cherline would like to get a driver's license, but she has no identification right now.

Carol says that when Cherline wanted to go to her prom, Voices for Kids, the nonprofit that supports the guardian ad litem program, came up with the money to buy Cherline a dress. Those funds were used to buy a blue, strapless gown that fit tall, thin Cherline like a dream. "It took this gangly kid and turned her into a princess, and she was just ravishingly beautiful," Bev says.

Both of Cherline's guardians share a deep affection for the quiet young woman. "She's a survivor," says Carol, "but the poem really reflects some of her sadness."

Why Do I Cry

I'm crying

Why am I crying

Would someone tell me why

Why do I cry

Is it because I want my mommy

Is it because I want my daddy

Is it because I'm sad

Is it because I'm mad

Why do I cry

I want a life

I need a family

I need to love

I need to be loved

Why do I cry

Someone help me

Get me out this misery

Someone please

Find out

—Cherline Norvilus

You ask,

"Why am I crying?"

I'll try to tell you why.

You cry because you're human.

And caring people cry.

You cry because you're feeling,

And it's normal to have fears.

The three Ts aid in healing—

Talking, Time and Tears.

So let those tears flow freely,

It's cleansing so they say.

And there must be some rain,

To enjoy a sunny day.

So believe in your tomorrows,

And look for rainbows in the sky,

And know my dear Cherline,

That it's okay to cry.

—Bev McFerren ✦

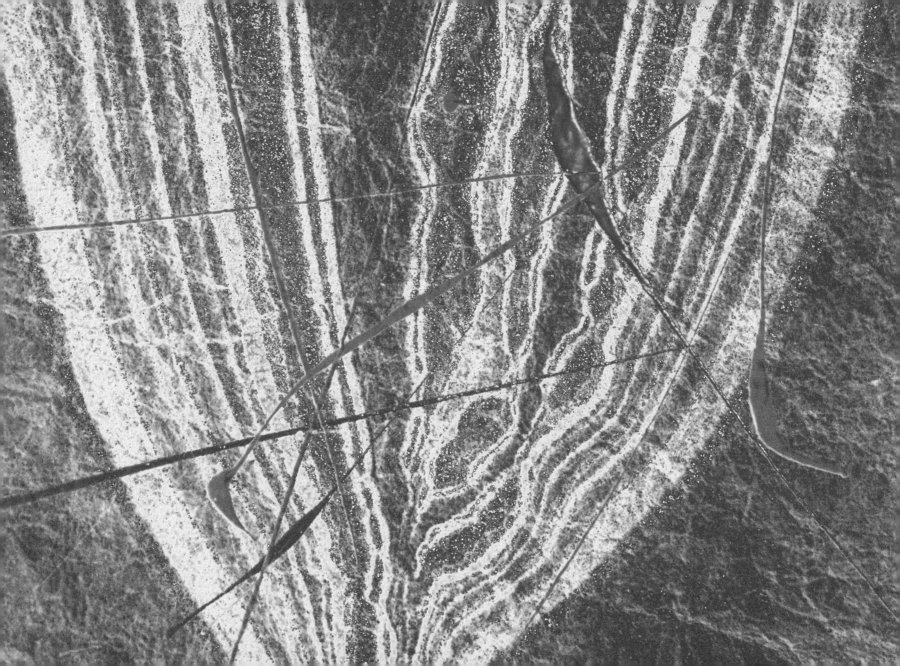

Joanna Patterson
South Bend, Indiana
CASA Program of St. Joseph County

Cheri Pomeroy began working with CASA after too often finding herself angry over news reports about abused and neglected children. She and her husband had sold a successful business and retired young, but instead of relaxing, Cheri is driving all over Indiana to visit the children involved in her cases. She has the right combination of compassion and grit to be a terrific advocate.

Cheri didn't think twice about making the drive to see Joanna Patterson when she was placed in a secure facility in Wabash, nearly two hours from South Bend. When she learned that Joanna's birthday was going to be unacknowledged while she was in Wabash, she brought the makings of a small birthday party to the facility.

Joanna and Cheri talk several times a month, and Cheri says she is trying to keep Joanna focused on school and making the right choices. "If you do the right thing, you can do the things you want," Cheri has always told Joanna. So when Joanna was told she couldn't go home for a long-planned visit to her foster family because the family was providing respite care that weekend for some teenage boys, Cheri wouldn't stand for it. "She hadn't done anything wrong," Cheri says of the situation. She felt Joanna's hard work and good grades in school should be rewarded as promised. Cheri kept making calls to the caseworker and eventually the caseworker's supervisor until another placement was found for the teenage boys for the weekend and Joanna was allowed to go home.

"All they want is someone they can count on," Cheri says of the young people she works with. "Everybody needs that."

My CASA Volunteer

Cheri is a person I look up to because of her honesty and kindness. She has helped me find a better future.

My name is Joanna Patterson. I am 14 years old and in the ninth grade. My CASA volunteer's name is Cheri. She has been my CASA for 11 months. Cheri is a person I look up to because of her honesty and kindness. She has helped me find a better future. She has always been there for me and always is on top of things when I need her. She is a parent figure in my life.

My sister Jackie and I are separated from each other in different towns. Cheri is the only one who comes and sees both of us. One time I had a home pass taken away for no reason, and Cheri made sure that I got it back so I could come home. It seems like whenever there is a problem she finds out what happened and gets it fixed for me.

She has done things for my sisters too. One time in court she asked that my sister be taken out of school because she was in trouble. My sister will be getting her GED next month. On my birthday, she brought my favorite cupcakes for everyone and a present for me. I thought that was very nice. That was the first time they had done that.

The other girls in my cottage wish they had a CASA. They hear what Cheri does for me and they like to talk to her when she comes to see me. I think it would be nice if everyone could have a CASA volunteer because she is my friend.

Chrystina Paolella
East Haven, Connecticut
Connecticut Department of Children and Families

When Chrystina Paolella got the entry form for the "Someone There for Me" essay contest, she says only one person came to mind, her social worker Zsuzsanna Papp.

According to Chrystina, Zsuzsanna is a caring, committed worker who despite a heavy caseload takes the extra time to make the children she works with feel special. "Each child has something that one can connect with," Zsuzsanna says. "I try to find that something." In Chrystina she saw strength, intelligence, and an articulate and assertive young woman who needed encouragement and care.

In her many years in the foster care system, Chrystina, now 15, was bounced from foster homes to shelters to hospitals to residential placements. She says it was Zsuzsanna who made her feel loved and kept her from despairing after yet another placement went awry.

Christina also clung to school, where she is a strong student and a prolific writer. She says her poems and stories usually come out right the first time she writes them down. Her crisp, grammatical essay for the contest took her only 45 minutes to write. "School is my thing," Chrystina says, but she admits that her common sense doesn't always match her book smarts. "I've made some bad choices."

Chrystina was recently adopted and changed her name from Alexandra when the process was finalized. She says it symbolizes a new beginning.

My Angel

A lot of the placements I was in were very bad.
Some were filthy; some parents were not fit to have kids,
and some I left because I was emotionally unstable.
I figured the world hated me.

When I first heard about the contest a few minutes ago from my DCF worker, Zsuzsanna Papp, I was solely concerned about prizes and money. However, after spending a while thinking about the essay, I had a different point of view. Suddenly, the last 11 years of my life flashed before my eyes.

Since I do not know much about my GAL and I had an attorney, I wanted to write about someone much more important to me. Previous to my being adopted by my current placement, I was in about 30 homes, hospitals, and shelters, almost all of which I was in for less than six months. A lot of the placements I was in were very bad. Some were filthy; some parents were not fit to have kids, and some I left because I was emotionally unstable. I figured the world hated me.

Then, in 1997, things started looking up. My social worker Michelle got married and left me with a new woman. Her name was Zsuzsanna. Zsuzsanna did a lot for me. She treated me as if I was her own child and sometimes I think she even forgot I wasn't.

During the holidays, she got me presents and told me she cared. The things I like most about her though were not the materialistic aspects of our relationship but the emotional bond we shared.

Sometimes, if I got kicked out of a placement for bad behavior to the extent that the people would not keep me any longer, I waited out the day in her office being spoiled while she frantically explained to prospective placements what a good girl I was. She lectured me sometimes, but she was never really angry with me. She was always gentle and never malicious with anything she said.

If she took me to visit with my mother or sister, I could always count on a drive to the nearest McDonald's to be spoiled afterwards. It might not be appropriate for social worker to become so attached to their cases that they express in words that they love them, but Zsuzsanna made me feel special. The way she said it always made me feel happy and wanted. At times I'm pretty sure I even asked her if she could adopt me.

With every home I went to she assured me that this one would be "the one," and after I had left it for one reason or another she would tell me I'd move on to bigger and better things.

She never doubted the fact I could make something of myself. She always encouraged me to be good and get good grades and assured me I would go to college if I wanted to. I know what I have said is not much but it means a lot to me. If she hadn't been as kind and hadn't pushed me as much as she has I wouldn't be where I am today.

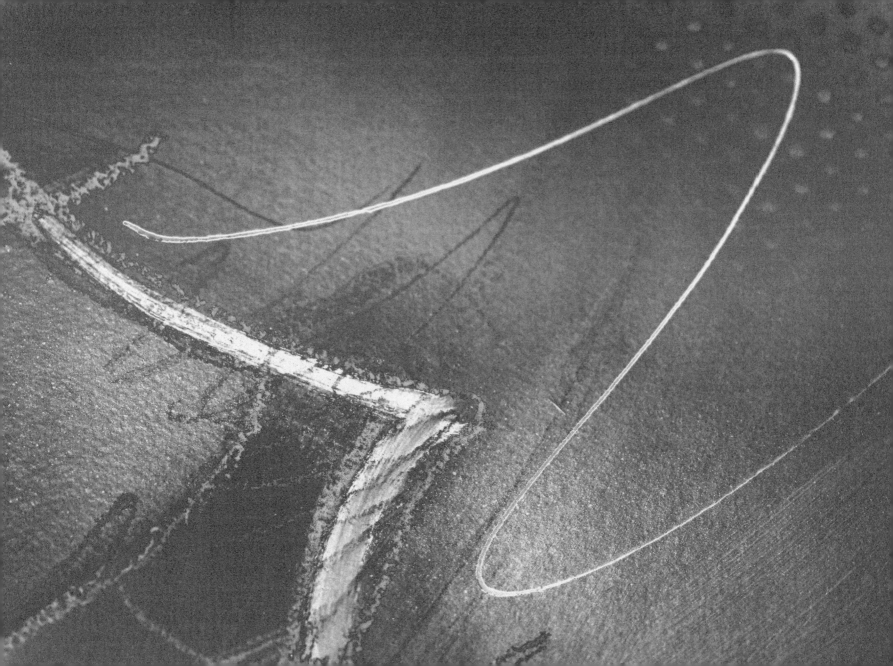

Shamor Santrell Peeler
Hickory, North Carolina
25th Judicial District of North Carolina Guardian ad Litem Program

"No child should have a thick file," says guardian ad litem volunteer Angela Phillips when asked to reflect on 14-year-old Shamor Peeler. The affection she has for the teen pulses through her words, as does her hurt and frustration that Shamor has been shuffled around by the system and had so many disappointments. Shamor has been through several adoption attempts that failed because the adoptive family moved or got pregnant or simply changed their minds. A string of dark luck that Angela says has nothing to do with the intelligent, articulate, and artistic boy they were considering bringing into their homes.

Angela admits that her seven-year role as Shamor's guardian has been longer and more intense than the position is designed to be or than she ever expected. But in a childhood that has been filled by many caseworkers, therapists, and attorneys and even more placements, Angela has been Shamor's most steadfast resource, advocate, and friend. "If he needed something for school or wanted piano lessons or piano books then I would go to the community and get those funds—go to churches and other community groups to make sure he has birthday presents and Christmas presents," Angela says. "It was a wraparound for him. To provide the things the system could not and would not provide." Shamor says Angela is his confidante and fills a role he can't quite find words for. "We're like...I call her my mom now," he says.

Angela says Shamor has a compassion that is rare for someone so young. "He can focus intently on other people and their pain," she says. Shamor is also a gifted musician and a strong tennis player. He excels in school and has a great sense of humor. Angela recently helped Shamor get into skating lessons and he has shined at that as well. He is now in the highest level of lessons and is doing double axels and sit spins. "He has an unusual resilience," says Angela. "He was just born with a resilience."

How the GAL Program Has Helped Me

She told me no matter what that she cared for me.
That made a difference in my life. For the first time in a long time,
I knew that somebody actually cared about me.

Hi. My name is Shamor, and I am a 14-year-old boy who loves to have fun. Unfortunately the events in my life have not all been fun and games. I have been in DSS custody since I was six weeks old. My GAL has helped me throughout these last several years. My GAL's name is Angela Hendrix Phillips. She helps me get through the hard times in life. I honestly love her to death. I call her my "White Mama" because I am black, but she treats me as if I was her own son.

You might wonder how she has helped me. Ever since I was 8 years old she has helped me in every way she possibly can. I remember when I was just starting puberty, Angela sat me down and explained to me what in the world was going on with my body. I still thank her to this day for that. I don't know what I would do without her. She is sweet, kind, and she does her best. Sometimes I sit down and wonder why she keeps on giving me the things I need even when I am a real jerk. Trust me on this one, I can be a jerk. One day I figured out it was because she truly cares for the children that she helps. She doesn't do

it for the money because there are jobs that pay much more than hers for the degree she has.

About a month ago, I was down and out. I felt that I needed to commit suicide. She told me no matter what that she cared for me. That made a difference in my life. For the first time in a long time I knew that somebody actually cared about me. Eventually, I turned my life around. After about a month, I realized that I needed motivation. My motivation was ice skating. I had no ice skates and no suits to skate in. I only had $30 and wanted lessons that cost $64. In case you don't know, skating is not cheap. Angela told me that if I could look forward to something I can achieve it. She gave me the tool that was missing from my toolbox, and she helped me get skating lessons. She not only did her job, but she went the extra mile.

She not only does "material" things for me. She gives me the emotional and mental support I need. I have gone through five failed adoptions. I didn't give myself any credit for trying to make the adoptions work. After the last one, I cried for two days straight. Angela told me that it wasn't my fault. She made me realize that even though I tried, I can't make people do anything. I had no hope at all. Angela helped me get the hope that I needed. I refused to go forward with another adoption. She told me to stop my self-pity and have some hope. It took me a while to realize that this was the truth and that I needed to do exactly what she advised. Now I am advocating for other children to get adopted. Children need families. Unfortunately, children cannot just dream up the perfect family and have that family ensure their safety. I am attempting to proceed into another adoption with a new attitude.

Hopefully, you now see how having a GAL has helped me improve my life. I hope I did her justice in this essay because there are so many things she does for me and other children. She is truly an inspiration. She has greatly influenced my life. Hopefully I can inspire other to believe in their selves the way Angela has believed in me. Remember, you can't achieve what you don't believe.

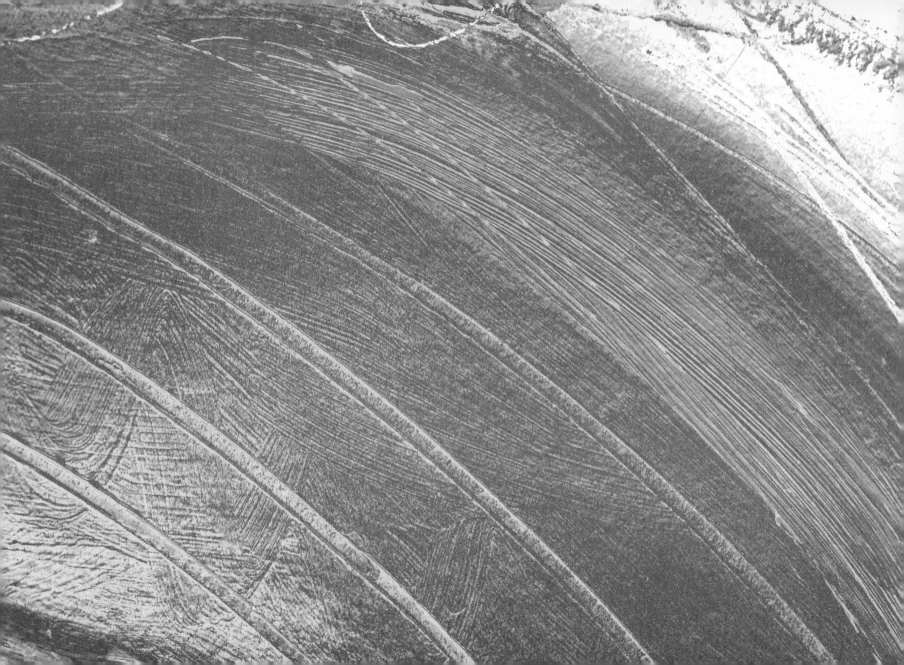

Jonnye Nicole Popick
San Marcos, California
Mentor

"I had to build my own family," says 18-year-old Jonnye Popick. She was removed from her birthhome at age 12 and feels entering the system saved her life and gave her the space she needed to separate her problems from those of her family. But entering the system also left holes in her support system—holes Jonnye tried to fill with caring, positive people. She says she had good social workers and an amazing attorney. She still keeps in touch with her judge and also learned to rely on the advice and support of her mentor Pat Tackett.

Pat is a professor in the psychology department at San Diego State University, and the lecture hall of her Adolescent Psychology course is filled every year with young adults with plans to become teachers, counselors, and therapists. Pat feels it is extremely important to expose her students to the real world and real kids, so each semester she puts together a panel of teens in the foster care system to speak with her class. Jonnye was one of the youth on that panel. Pat was impressed by her intelligence and later asked to serve as her mentor when she began working with a couple of other young women at Jonnye's school. Jonnye says Pat was always there for her to talk to and helped her focus on her goals.

"Jonnye is very independent, very strong willed, and super bright," Pat says. "But she needs guidance in using her strengths." Pat has learned in her years of study and practice that when working with adolescents, progress often comes slowly or haltingly. She tries to pass the message onto students who want to work with teens that they have to be understanding, patient, and satisfied with small steps. But even small steps can sometimes make a big difference.

When You Lose Hope...

The days that I cried she was there or on the other line telling me that things were going to be okay. She made me feel I was somebody every time I talked to her.

Have you ever thought that you will never be able to love someone? Love yourself? Be somebody? Then all of a sudden when you are at your lowest, you get introduced to someone who touches your life forever?

I have been there. I have come from the lowest of the low; thinking that there wasn't a chance for me to survive. Then my mentor, Pat Tackett, came into my life. She helped me see a future with love, happiness, and success. She guided me to set goals and have the faith that I never thought I would have again.

I remember the first time I met my mentor. I was at my group home. She came volunteering to do sex education. I thought she was the most straightforward person in the world. I admired that, but I didn't want to let my guard down. I left the group to attend an academy. I hoped I would see her again but didn't know if I would. Then one day she was there, and she asked if she could mentor me. I was so happy. One day we went to dinner, and I told her my goals and the struggles that I had in life with family and just with me. I felt like she

understood everything I was going through. I was amazed that she didn't judge me for the mistakes I have made in my life. The days that I cried she was there or on the other line telling me that things were going to be okay. She made me feel I was somebody every time I talked to her. She made me laugh and took me to her classes so I could get to know the college life. I was so excited. When I went to the college she taught at, I felt I had the chance to be like them. I had a chance to live a successful life that I never thought was possible. I had a couple dreams, but I didn't think they would become anything.

We set goals together, and, today, I am following them. I am going to Cal State San Marcos in the spring of 2004, and right now I work for a nonprofit organization for homeless and abused women and children. I am the operations manager. I still speak with her and get her assistance as needed and share my accomplishments with her.

I am grateful to have had her in my life, extremely grateful. Thank you to the mentoring program and God for bringing her back into my life.

Once You Get Strength

There was a young lady in my group home who had a lot of self-worth obstacles she needed to overcome. She was self-mutilating and just angry at the world. Every day she was putting someone down. I definitely saw myself in her. I knew she needed tough love and a good friend. In the beginning she wasn't able to see that it wouldn't take her pain away if she hurt someone else. Every night, I would let her know that her pain wasn't the fault of other girls or the staff. And every time she hurt someone else she had to live with more guilt and sadness. I also always said, "Kelly, when you are ready, I am here."

One day she came to me and asked, "Jonnye, can we talk outside?" I was so excited that I stopped everything I was doing, and we went outside. We were outside about two hours talking about her struggles and fears and the faith she wished she had. I remember what she said with tears coming down, "I want to stop cutting, taking things out on others, get to know myself, and get my grades up." At the time we were both in tears.

We talked some more, hugged, and went into the house. That night we had a house meeting. During the meeting, she said she was going to need help from the whole house to call her on things when she is being disrespectful and understand that starting today she was going to find who she really is.

Even though we are both not at that group home, we still talk about our daily accomplishments and we've become a support team for one another. Now she also helps others. It is like a chain that can't be broken once it gets started.

Jamie Lee Porter
Kingsland, Texas
CASA for the Highland Lakes Area

On her final day in court before aging out of foster care in the summer of 2003, Jamie Porter asked if she could read something before her case was dismissed. Jamie's CASA volunteer Ann Ratisseau says everyone in the courtroom that day was just blown away by Jamie's eloquent letter, which is printed on the next page. Here was a young woman who had been through so much but had the maturity and strength to be self-reflective and hopeful on her last day in care.

When Ann met Jamie in January of 2001, the 15-year-old was dealing with a painful history of abuse and fragile mental health. Things would not get easier on Jamie as she was rotated through nine different placements. Ann made sure she visited Jamie at each new facility, and drove an hour and a half with balloons and a cake to brighten Jamie's hospital room on her 16th birthday. Several months later, Jamie was in a placement that was flooded, and she lost everything. Ann says Jamie's photo albums and journals and poetry were ruined, and she had to work with the school districts Jamie had been in to recreate academic records so Jamie could sign up to take her GED.

During her years in care, Jamie was also grappling with her sexuality, and it was Ann she finally turned to when she was ready to let people know she was gay. CASA volunteer supervisor Barbie Ott says Ann was the one person Jamie felt comfortable in telling. "Ann is just a calm, sure person," Barbie says. Ann encouraged Jamie to talk to her therapist and grow more comfortable with that part of her identity. Ann was also there to help Jamie set up her apartment when she moved into a transitional living facility.

Jamie was an intense case for Ann's first experience as a CASA volunteer, but Ann was willing to provide the support and guidance Jamie so needed to make some tough years a bit easier.

Aging Out

*These three years of being in the state's care have been the hardest but the most rewarding.
I walked many roads. I've been through things that I did not want to see or feel,
but that is what helped me find myself.*

I came into CPS custody in October 2000. I was scared and angry. I did not know what to do or think. I was a teen trying to find myself. Thoughts of suicide were passing through my head. I began to wonder if there was a God, and, if there was, I came to the conclusion that He wasn't so great. I cried tears from the inside, but I would not allow them to fall from my dull, hazel eyes. I was in search of something I could not describe. I wondered what was missing, but I couldn't figure it out. Was it my misunderstanding of one or all? I didn't know. I wondered if I was meant to live. I love my dad and stepmom to death, but I realized there was a different way of life in our minds and that worried me. I though maybe if I died, the battle of misunderstanding would end. I was hurting from years of pain that I could not describe. I felt an anger in me that I did not want, but it was taking over me. I was a teen looking for hope and love. I had so many thoughts crossing my teenage mind. I was trying to figure out what to do. I have a determination that will not die, and I believe that this is what kept me

alive. I had always had a dream of being somebody. The one thing that held me back was fear.

These three years of being in the state's care have been the hardest but the most rewarding. I walked many roads. I've been through things that I did not want to see or feel, but that is what helped me find myself. I had a struggle with spirituality, I overcame my depression, and I learned to talk about my problems and believe in myself and God. Most of all, I learned to love, forgive, and care for others. I stepped out from behind my wall of insecurities. But I did not do this alone. Thanks to my caseworker and the staff of every place I have been, but especially thanks to Ann Ratisseau, I found myself.

Ann has been with me and stuck with me through thick and thin. When I first met her, I knew that she would be a stepping stone in my life. She believed in me when nobody else did. I could cry to her and not feel ashamed. We built a strong friendship and family-ship. We had our laughs and our tough times. She helped me out with anything

I needed. She comes and sees me on my birthdays and other important holidays. Sometimes, she just comes to come. CASA couldn't have selected a better volunteer for their program. I will miss Ann, but she will always be a part of my life. In my eyes, she will always be a part of my family.

One question I asked myself while I was in the state's care is whether my father will be proud of me by the time this is over. His answer, I hope, will be yes. I love my dad. I always have, and I always will. Now we can talk without having an argument.

Since 2000, I furthered my education. I found myself and was able to stabilize my emotions. I found a strong faith in God. I went through a huge spiritual struggle. I just didn't understand God, and I finally figured out that you can believe in things you don't understand. I actually started to live outside my world in the real world. I learned that everything will come in time if it is meant to be. I also learned to always have faith. I'm sad that I'm aging out of care, but I will continue the adult program, and Preparation for Adult Living will pay for some of my vocational school. I just want to say thank you for your support and love. All of you turned me into a successful young woman.

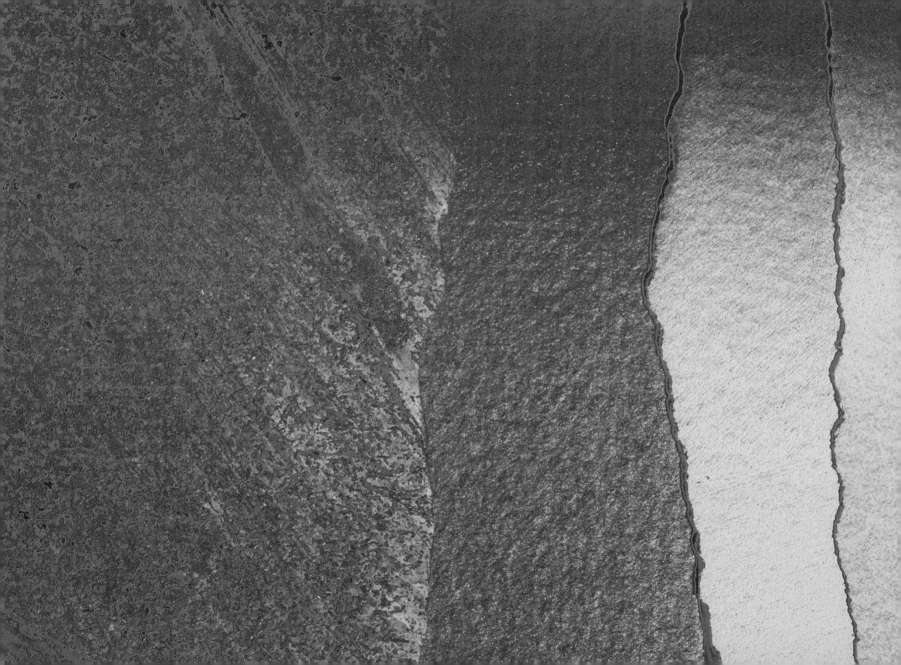

Ashley Rhodes-Courter
Crystal River, Florida
Guardian ad Litem Program—13th Judicial Circuit

Volunteer guardian ad litem Mary Miller has already made 17-year-old Ashley Rhodes-Courter promise her center row seats on the day Ashley makes her Broadway debut. Mary has no doubt the day will come and says Ashley is a gifted actress who does a dead-on, hilarious Lucille Ball imitation.

For Ashley, acting is a pride and a passion, but she admits some of her talent was cultivated through pain and the self-protecting desire to escape from the reality of her life. "I've always loved it," Ashley says of acting. "Maybe it's the element of being on stage and being in the spotlight, and not being yourself." She says she always loved anything that dealt with make believe; anything that let her pretend her world was different than it was.

Ashley came into care when she was 2 as a result of her mother's substance abuse. And at a young age, Ashley took over the role of protector and parent for her young brother. The siblings were living in a group home where Mary was working with another child, when she asked to be appointed to their case. But five years in the system had already taken a toll on then 8-year-old Ashley. "I didn't trust her," Ashley says frankly. "She was just another adult in my life making promises that I didn't quite believe." A convincing performance for Ashley meant more than reading from the script, it meant putting the force of actions and emotional commitment behind the lines. And Mary more than met the standard.

Ashley says Mary became the only stable adult in her life and followed her as she moved from placement to placement. When Ashley told her about a dangerous, abusive foster home, Mary tried to get it closed. When Ashley's brother was placed back in that home, Mary made regular calls and visits to the foster home to make sure he was safe and worked tirelessly to get him moved. "I'm just a bulldog by nature," Mary says. In this case, her nature paid off in a successful and happy adoption for Ashley after too many years in flux.

Bright and extremely articulate, Ashley now has almost two years of college credit completed. She has stayed technically enrolled in high school to remain in drama and to serve as drama club president, but all of her classes are at a local community college, and she works hard to juggle both responsibilities. But in spite of all of her talent and success, neat and happy endings are harder to achieve in real life than they are on stage. Ashley says, "I don't really open up to people." It took the teen a long time to tell her adoptive parents that she loves them, and she still keeps most people at a distance. But she says her scars also fuel her art. "I have the background to understand when a character is in pain. I'm able to tap into my life experiences."

Lost in the System—Found by a CASA Volunteer

Mary attended all of the Children's Home events.
When she was around cheering me on, I felt like I had my own private fan club.
Behind the scenes she was working on finding a family for me.

I like to think that my story has three parts. First is the time when I felt like I was lost in the foster care system. Second is when my guardian ad litem, Mary Miller, came into my life. And third is when she helped find a family for me.

Due to my mother's problems with substance abuse, I was placed in foster care when I was 2 and a half. I lived in some homes for a few days, others a few weeks or months. Most were kind and tried to care for me, but one was horrendous. They had as many as 16 foster kids, including a lot of babies, in a trailer with only three bedrooms. I was there when I was 7 and 8, and I had to diaper and care for the babies. But the worst moments were the really cruel punishments, like having to run laps in the hot sun, crouching in awkward positions, being hit with a spoon until my bottom was raw, and having food withheld. My brother, who is younger and has Attention-Deficit/Hyperactivity Disorder, had his head dunked in the bathtub until he almost drowned and had hot sauce poured down his throat. Eventually, the family was

investigated. They denied everything so I was branded a troublemaker and sent to a shelter home, leaving my brother behind.

A few months later we were reunited in a better foster home. Since we had no CASA volunteer, Mary Miller, who was already representing another child in this home, agreed to take us on as well. I'd like to say that Mary and I became best friends, but by then I already had eight foster mothers, a birthmother, my grandfather's girlfriend, not to mention shifts of counselors in the shelter, and, although Mary was nice enough, I didn't expect her to make a difference. Why should I? Nobody else ever had.

After I told Mary Miller what happened at the abusive foster home, she began her own investigation. And she also tried to get me back some of my precious things, including a special doll that the foster home had kept. Later, when my brother and I had to change placements once again, they sent me to one home and my brother back to the abusive home. Mary was so afraid he would be harmed again that she kept going to their home and calling to check on him. Thirteen days later, they let him go. Then Mary worked to get their home closed.

It took two years, but finally their license was revoked. Unfortunately, the Department of Children and Family allowed that family to adopt seven of the children in the home. Then, about three years ago, Mary Miller called with startling news. That family had been arrested for more than 30 counts of felony child abuse with torture. Nobody believed me then, but they did now.

While I dreamed of a family I could call my own, Mary Miller was working to get me free for adoption. My mother refused to give me up or do her case plan, but Mary attended every hearing and was there every time my mother was arrested. At one point, after my mother was released from mandatory drug testing, Mary asked her to take another drug test to prove the she was serious about wanting me back. She refused and signed the papers instead. After nothing had been done in my case for five years, Mary managed all of this in five months. My birthmother claimed she didn't know who my father was, but Mary was able to get his rights terminated seven months after she took the case.

Mary concluded that the Children's Home would be the best placement for us, but we needed all sorts of recommendations and exams, which Mary helped arrange. I know for a fact that if she hadn't followed through on every detail, nothing would have ever changed. And this time, when a foster parent tried to keep my blue bike, Mary got it back for me!

Mary attended all of the Children's Home events. When she was around cheering me on, I felt like I had my own private fan club. Behind the scenes she was working on finding a family for me. When my adoptive mother and father started looking for a child, they heard about me from someone who had visited the Children's Home. They called the adoption department several times, but got the run around. It was when they met Mary that things began to happen. Finally, on July 28, 1998, we went to court for the adoption. Of course, Mary Miller was there. Now I have two birthdays every year: November 22 and July 28. I'd like to see a lot more children like me having two days to celebrate. Only nobody should have to wait almost 10 years for a permanent family. If I had been given a volunteer from the moment I went into the system, many mistakes could have been prevented. The truth is that it was only when I was assigned a guardian that things began to change, but it still took three long years from when Mary Miller met me until I was adopted.

Many people are ignorant about what foster children can achieve. Luckily my CASA volunteer had great expectations for me! But while I wouldn't want anyone else to go through what I did, even when I felt all alone and lost I imagined a life like the one I am living. I never realized what it would take to make it reality, but I'm certainly glad my guardian ad litem did. I probably haven't thanked Mary properly. So thank you Mary Miller for everything. Without you, I don't know where I would be today.

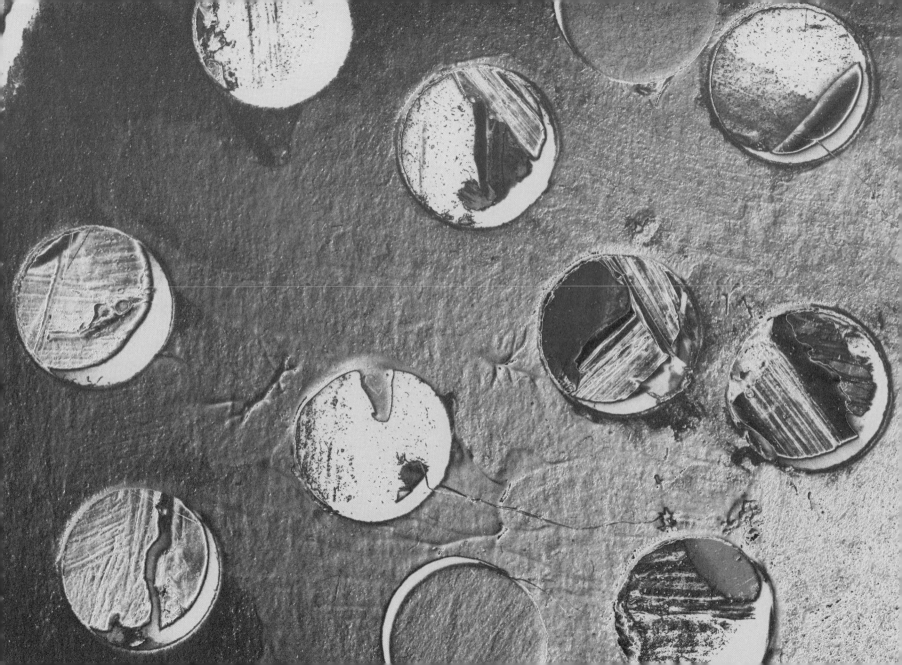

Lindsey Shorter
Carrollton, Georgia
Carroll County CASA

Lindsey Shorter, 14, is the third generation in her family to be involved in the child welfare system. Her caseworker, Ruth Reid, says the system is Lindsey's family history, but it does not have to be her legacy. "Lindsey can break the cycle," Ruth says. The dedicated caseworker feels that the caring, personable young woman just needs a positive role model to help bring out her strengths and keep her focused on her goals.

For more than three years, that role model has been CASA volunteer Emily Cole. Emily was in the second class of volunteers at the Carroll County CASA in Georgia, which began taking cases in 1999. Program Director Amanda Camp says Emily has been recognized as volunteer of the year while she was also juggling a career and raising two sons. Because Lindsey has lived so much of her childhood in foster care, moving from home to home, Emily has concentrated most on bringing focus, stability, and support into Lindsey's life.

With all of the moves she's been through, Lindsey has never stayed in the same classroom for an entire year, and her progress in school has understandably suffered. To help boost her reading and math skills, Emily ensures she gets to tutoring twice a week. She says it is one of the ways she reinforces for Lindsey that she is there for her and believes in her. "The small things show me that this child has so much potential," Emily says.

Lindsey has just started an independent living program, and Ruth wants to see Lindsey and a few others in her caseload make it through the system before she retires. The teen loves animals, and Emily is encouraging her to work toward her dream of being a veterinarian or veterinarian's assistant and is working to find a vet's office in which Lindsey can volunteer. More important, Emily has let Lindsey know she's behind her as she spends her last years in the foster care system and prepares for independence. "Lindsey knows that wherever she goes, I'll always be there for her," Emily says. That alone may mean the difference between an old cycle continuing or a new one beginning with Lindsey.

Lindsey and Emily: Good Friends

Emily always tells me she loves me, and she always encourages me to do my best.

My name is Lindsey, and I had my 14th birthday this month. I have been in foster care for a large portion of my life. The last time I came into foster care, a CASA volunteer was appointed for me. Her name is Emily. Emily always brings me homemade cookies. The cookies are always really good. My favorite ones are the chocolate chip. The first time I met Emily, she came with my caseworker to move me to my new foster home. While at that foster home, she walked with me to Dairy Queen and we had a Blizzard. That was my first Blizzard. The walk was long, but we had fun talking. For my birthday that year, she arranged with my caseworker for us to be able to have a special lunch together with my sister. When I moved from that foster home, Emily helped me write a thank you note to that foster parent for helping me with my manners and behavior.

Emily continued to be there for me. She visited me at school and sometimes would bring lunch for us. In September 2001, the judge decided that I would not be allowed to go back home to my mother. I talked with my school counselor about my future and told her that I knew Emily loved me and would always be there for me. And she has. Since that time, I have been in some foster homes that were far away from where Emily lives. But she always comes to see me and brings me cookies. She always remembers my birthday, and we celebrate it together. Emily always tells me she loves me, and she always encourages me to do my best. When I moved to my aunt and uncle's house it was hard starting off. When I had problems, I could call her and we would talk about them together. Talking about my problems to Emily helped me. So I try to help other foster youth by talking to them. Most foster youth don't have a CASA volunteer to talk to like I do. One foster girl who I lived with was having a really hard time and wanted to go home. I encouraged her to pray and hope for the best that maybe she would be able to go home. And she did. I help my sister, Jessica, a lot. She wants very much to be able to see our mother. I encourage her to pray that one day, when we are older, that we will be able to see our mother and that our mother will be healthy and remember the good times we had together. I encourage my foster friends to pray because I find that praying is helpful. I have an idea to help another young person. I have long hair, and I have been thinking about getting it cut. Emily has told me about a way to donate my cut hair to help make hair pieces for children who have lost their hair because of cancer. I know that these children might not be foster children, but they would be children who are in need, and this would be a way that I could help.

Meagan and Christin Stegall
Carrollton, Georgia
DeKalb County CASA

CASA volunteer Linda Stacy was poring over the case file for the three Stegall sisters, trying to learn all she could about their history. In the file, she found several phone numbers and old messages left with caseworkers. Not knowing where the numbers would lead her, she just started dialing.

The sisters had come into care after Meagan, the oldest, took the brave step of telling a teacher that everything wasn't okay at home. Linda says the girls didn't know they had an extended family and had spent months in shelters and group homes before she got their case. The first time she met the girls, Linda says they gave her a look that said, "Oh no, here comes another stranger into our lives." The stress in their faces was palpable. She got to know them slowly by just spending time and taking walks with them through the Atlanta neighborhoods near their group home.

As it turned out, the numbers Linda found in the file led her to the girls' great-aunt who had been trying to track them down. Just a few months after Linda took the case, their aunt began the process of getting legal custody of the girls. "That case made me realize how much a CASA volunteer can help," says Linda, who feels passionately about her role as a volunteer. "This is the path I'm supposed to be taking."

Christin and Meagan have settled into life with their great-aunt, and Linda says they are both blossoming and doing well in school. Their aunt, a slip of a woman with a heart big enough to welcome in the three sisters along with her own six children, has given them stability and a sense of home. Linda says, "I wish I could have taken a picture to show then and now."

Thick and Thin

By Meagan Stegall

From the start, we could tell she was going to be with us through thick and thin.

First, I would like to introduce myself. My name is Meagan Stegall, and I am writing this essay on my CASA volunteer, Mrs. Linda Stacy. She's a great woman and an even better CASA. She is still a very special person to me and always will be. I love her very much and always will.

Mrs. Linda Stacy has always been there for me and my sisters. If I was stressed out about an upcoming court date, school grades, or family problems she would offer her shoulder or a hug. I have always had her there when I needed someone to fall back on. She was my support and motivation; always cheering me to go on and always bringing out the good in all the situations that were bad and depressing.

I remember the day we were at the Sam Bell group home like it was yesterday. I thought she was just another person who would leave or walk out when the work load is too much to bear, or who wouldn't stay when she didn't want to put up with all the problems the case brought. But from the start, we could tell she was going to be with us through thick and thin.

When you are in foster care it's really hard to trust somebody, but I have trusted Mrs. Linda Stacy. She was like the mom I never really had. But she was always correcting my mistakes and teaching me to respect family values. She would also teach me what I wanted to know about anything. She also always told me the truth. She would never "beat around the bush." She would tell us what was happening up front. My sisters and I really respected that. We were not always happy about situations, but we were informed.

I really don't know if I would be able to do some of the things she has done for me and my sisters. She was always looking out for us and thinking about how she could make us feel better. A CASA volunteer is a very special person. Not just anyone could be a CASA and do half as well as Mrs. Linda Stacy did, because she really loves and cares.

I am thinking now about some life goals. I really think I want to be a teacher so I can teach children and care for them at the same time. I really haven't thought about becoming a CASA, but it is something I am going to strongly consider. If I decide it is something I want to do and will be good at, I hope I will make a great impact on a child's life like Mrs. Linda Stacy has done on mine. I will never forget all she did for me and my sisters. She was one of the blessings God has given me. I love her very much and I hope more people like her will decide to be a CASA volunteer. When they finish the case, they will really see that all the work was worth it.

A Great Role Model

By Christin Stegall

When we needed anything she was there.

Mrs. Linda Stacy helped me get over all the little flashbacks that I had. She took the time to come and talk with me and my other two sisters. When we needed anything she was there. She always had a positive attitude. She was a great role model. She loved to come and talk with me and my sisters.

If I was to have any CASA volunteer I'm glad it was her. Best wishes to whoever gets her next because she is so sweet.

Timothy Wellbaum
Lima, Ohio
Shelby County CASA/GAL

First-time guardian ad litem volunteer Diana Morrow was handed a thick file when she got the case of 16-year-old Timothy Wellbaum and an earful about what to expect from the teen. Tim's family has a long history with the child welfare system, and he had acted out as a youth. Diana listened to what she was told and took a look at the case file, and then cleared it from her mind. She says she went to visit Tim for the first time with the mindset, "I'm going to start with who I see now."

"When I met him, he wasn't at all what I was led to expect," Diana says. The Tim she got to know was very mature, intelligent, and sensitive.

The teen had been accused of a crime and was moved from a group home into a more secure facility. Diana says the case against him was slim and he was never adjudicated, but the system was ready to treat him like he was a criminal. She said it was working on this case that made her understand why the volunteer guardian ad litem program is so vital. "This case needed fresh eyes," she says.

Diana started visiting Tim weekly at the secure facility and talking to him about his case. "I think he needed someone to believe in him," she says. "To see him as he saw himself."

Diana worked to get an attorney appointed to Tim and then worked to get the case the attention she felt it deserved. Diana says being a first-time volunteer worked in her favor in Tim's case. "I had an advantage in that I was going to do what seemed right until someone told me I couldn't do that."

Her aggressive approach worked, and the judge insisted Tim be moved from the secure facility into a foster home. By this time, the young man had turned 17 and needed time to prepare for being on his own. He is now finishing a vocational high school where he is learning floral design. Tim says Diana was not only a terrific advocate but a great comfort to him. "She was really there to help and listen and share moments of her childhood."

Diana says she and Tim both learned greater strength and patience by working together on his case. "I found him very inspiring."

It's So True That They Are Your Friend

Within a month's time she was working tireless nights with my lawyer.
He seemed as if he was not interested, but she was not accepting that.

It all started around February 2003 when my caseworkers came to me and told me that a GAL was appointed to me. She knew nothing of me, and, since I was in a group home, maybe she wondered. But the first time she came to see me she was very open and willing to learn about me. It seemed as if we shared the same thoughts and part of my life. Around March we got the news that the group home I was in was closing for financial reasons. Then, one Thursday afternoon, I received a telephone call. It was the county telling me I was going to a locked facility. I was very upset about it. I called my GAL and told her how I was feeling. She seemed very understanding. Not knowing what was going to happen next seemed to feel better because my GAL made me feel safe.

In March, I had an appointment in Lima where my other facility was, and my GAL came with me. We got there and told them what was going on. They were all willing to help. I was amazed and so was my GAL. The next morning I woke up and called my GAL. She told me she had an appointment with the judge that morning. She presented the case to him with very little help. After she described my case to the judge, he appointed me a lawyer. I was happy. Soon after that I was placed in a program that was very strict—locked down and closed. I was very scared. My GAL came up every Tuesday. She never missed a day and for that I trusted her so much. Within a month's time she was working tireless nights with my lawyer. He seemed as if he was not interested, but she was not accepting that. She still worked hard and finally my lawyer got interested. So, while I was at this place, I received another phone call from my GAL. She told me that I had a court date set up. When my court date came—it was May 20th at 9:00 in the morning—my mom, my GAL, my lawyer, and I were all there for a full day in court. I was very amazed by how my GAL presented my case. It was like she knew me. Some of the things that others were saying were not true.

It was as if she had a baseball bat and was scoring home runs with those lies. She stood very strong and not one thing got left out. It was the first time I've ever seen someone stand up for what they believe.

Then came my second court date, and another full day in court. This was the one where the other side tried to prove their case. As my GAL learned more and more, she started to speak about me like I was her son. That day in court I was very scared not knowing what was going to happen, but she kept a smile on her face the whole time. Court was just about over when the judge said it was court ordered to move me to a foster home. We won the case. Wow. I learned some very good lessons out of this. I never thought I could actually stand up for my-self, but, through the whole thing, she made sure I could. Now I am a very strong person, and I don't let many things float away from me. I am so glad that I got appointed a GAL. I never had someone so close to me. I am actually glad that there was someone out there who spoke my mind and knew exactly what I was thinking. Since then, I've helped so many other kids. For example, the kids who are around me see that your mind can be positive and you shouldn't let any one say some-thing to you that is not true. I thank God each day that there is GAL because they are true friends. And, a word to the wise, you might think that GAL will try to take a family part in your child's life, but GAL is just another friend for you. I hope that you will support GAL for your child.

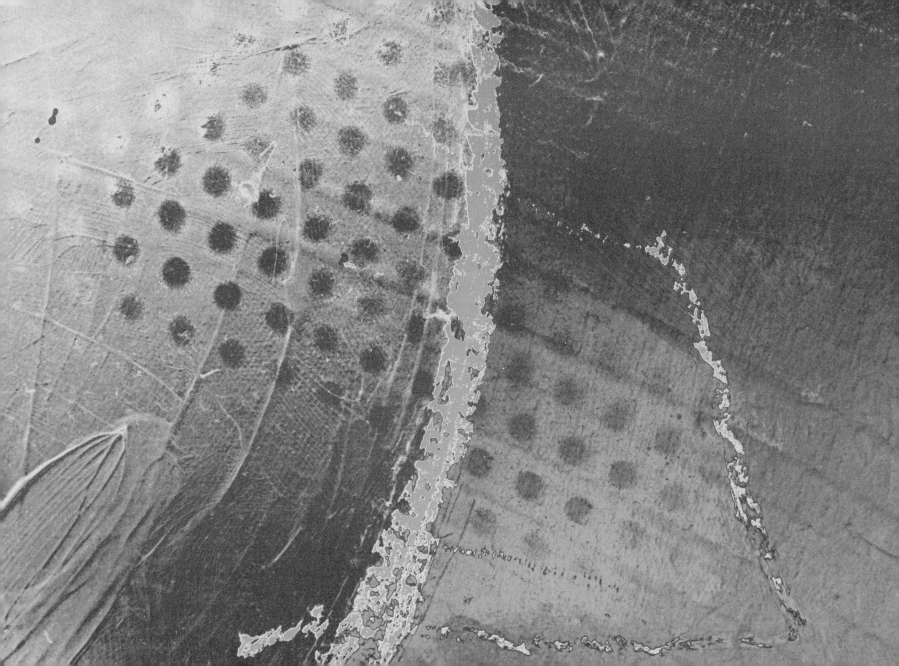

Meghan W.
Cambridge, Massachusetts
CASA of New Hampshire

Meghan W. admits that she didn't make things easy in the beginning for her CASA volunteer Karen Black.

Hurt, betrayed, and bounced around, 16-year-old Meghan was a young woman in such intense internal pain that she found some level of relief in inflicting physical harm on herself. Meghan worked temporarily with CASA volunteer supervisor Kathy Vachon until Karen was appointed to her case. Although Kathy stayed closely involved, Meghan says that when she met Karen she was mad that her CASA volunteer had switched and mad that she had to deal with yet another person coming into her life. "Every time, I did stuff to push her away," Meghan, now 20, says looking back. "I would yell at her; call her names. Not talk when she tried to talk to me." Fortunately, Karen wasn't easy to scare away. She just kept coming to visit as Meghan was moved more than a dozen times. "She was all over the state," says Karen. "It just kept shocking her that I kept showing up." Karen says the next step forward came when Meghan learned she was a volunteer; that she had chosen to spend the time with her.

Meghan wrote the letter printed on the next page about a year after she met Kathy and Karen. Kathy said she was without words when she read Meghan's emotional note. "She was just really struggling with what was good in her life," Kathy says. Karen says it was something that brought the two another step closer and into a more emotional relationship. Meghan handed her the note after a visit, and Karen read it on her way home. Weeping, she turned around and went back to Meghan's group home to wrap her arms around her.

Karen says Meghan has grown so much healthier, stronger, and more confident since she wrote that letter. "What's changed? My whole self," Meghan says. She believes it is remarkable that she is alive today and starting college. "If I didn't have them," Meghan says of Kathy and Karen, "I don't know where I'd be. They mean so much more now."

Dearest
Karen and Kathy

I walk every day in fear and caution of people,
trying to protect something that's already broken down inside me.

I was reading an article from *People Magazine* (January 24, 2000) called "Last Embrace." It's about a woman in California who won't let babies found dead and abandoned die unmourned and anonymous. It was a sad yet happy article. There was one statement this woman said that made me cry. The statement was, "I represent the child."

Even though what she does is very different from what you do, in a way it's the same. I just read this article and it's 2:15 A.M. (I have trouble falling asleep.) It made me think of you. As tears streamed down my face, I wanted to write you this letter, and I couldn't wait until I went to sleep and then woke up in the later morning to write it.

You know right now I'm almost 17. I'm trying so hard to keep myself alive. I constantly think about trying to kill myself. I look at where I am in life, compared to the normal 17-year-old girl. My mind isn't constantly on boys—wondering if I'll have a date to this or that or who I'll go to the junior prom with. Calling my friends and talking on the phone for long periods of time about nothing that REALLY matters in life isn't part of my daily living.

Instead of doing those things, I often sit in the bathroom or bedroom of my placement homes and cry for long periods of time, so lonely and confused about my past, present, and future. I sit in my self-pity party, and I cry for my mother who isn't and will never be there. I always have this false, unrealistic hope that maybe, just maybe someday she'll hold me in her arms like a little child, stroking my hair, consoling me and justifying why I cry.

I walk every day in fear and caution of people, trying to protect something that's already broken down inside me. And for what? It doesn't appear to even matter now, but it does, a lot. I try to find the perfect words to define how I feel, but I find none.

And then I have school. I want so badly to go to college and be somebody someday. But it seems to take more than I have or at least more than I can give out. I know I'm smart, but the recent trials of my life have taken the strength and effort that I need for school and my grades would show me as dumb.

I'm just sad, broken, and hurt. I feel chewed up and spit out. I'm confused about many things in my life, which seems so out of control. Why can't I do well in school? Why do they tell me "it's not your fault" yet everyday I live seems to be a punishment? Everyday I am moved around and played with as if I am just a pawn in a game of chess.

I want to thank you very much for understanding, and if not, at least trying to understand all the feelings and needs I have. And I want to thank you for representing the child (me) and trying to make this process as easy as possible for me. Thank you for taking my mother's place in protecting me and helping me prosper in life, when she has failed to do so. And even though it's your job, there is more to it. Thank you for caring and putting time into me. Thank you for helping me feel safer in the midst of what seems to be a civil war. Thanks for putting time into my life so that maybe someday I will be someone.

Afterword

To the Reader

Michael Piraino

I hope you were inspired by the stories you have read in this book. Take a moment now to think about one of the children about whom you've read. Imagine if someone had simply recited to you the facts of that child's maltreatment. You might have felt pessimistic about that child's future. We all hear repeatedly about the very real risks maltreated children face as they grow up. But each of the young people represented in this book is well on the way to a happy and productive life. They are an impressive group of people.

Each year, there are over half a million other abused and neglected children who could share stories that would sometimes sadden, but also often inspire you. Most of those stories will never be told publicly. Yet each one is made possible through the child's own strength of char-

acter, often supported through the involvement of a caring adult. For over a quarter million of these children, that adult is a CASA or guardian ad litem volunteer, but compassionate caseworkers, foster parents, lawyers, judges, and others also help fill this need.

All of these children, despite histories of abuse or neglect, are potential success stories. Whether and how well they succeed depends on the interplay of various risk and protective factors in their lives. Risk factors can include circumstances such as domestic violence, poverty, and poor parenting styles. New research has clearly confirmed that CASA volunteers are typically assigned to the most difficult cases, those with multiple risk factors for the children. This makes sense, since these are the cases where the child's ability to survive successfully is most in question.

As advocates for these children, our job might be described as changing the balance in favor of the protective factors. One of the most encouraging findings from researchers is that, if we pay enough attention to children, they can overcome many of the effects of even the most severe abuse. No child of any age is beyond helping, which is why CASA volunteers work with children from birth to 18, and sometimes beyond.

Research on children's resilience points out that we can affect children's lives even before achieving a dramatic reunification or adoption. One thing that comes through clearly in the stories in this book is the dramatic impact adults had on the children even before the court processes were concluded. A volunteer's presence can make children's lives better even in the absence of a permanent family, and regardless of what is happening in court.

Of course, our best outcomes are when we dramatically help to improve the child's safety through placement in a permanent home. But we must also remember that improving the out-of-home care experience itself helps makes children's lives better.

An important theme in both the research and the stories you have read is this: We need to maintain the quality of the work that is done on behalf of abused and neglected children. Quality produces better results. When their whole futures are at stake, as they can be in court proceedings related to abuse and neglect, children need adults to do all they can to protect, nurture, and understand them.

The CASA and guardian ad litem network has long had a reputation for quality. Courts, families, foster parents, children—the whole community, in fact—can be proud of the strength of the CASA network and the way it empowers quality volunteer advocacy for abused and neglected children.

Which brings me back to you, the reader of this book. If you are already involved, I thank you for the many ways you have been a part of children's success stories.

For readers not yet involved, if these stories inspired you, if they made you feel you'd like to be part of this important work for children, please consider volunteering or otherwise supporting the CASA network. The experience will be a powerful one. Your life may change as much as the children for whom you advocate.

CASA and volunteer guardian ad litem programs in over 975 communities stand ready to welcome your involvement. Contact us today at the addresses listed in the next section.

If you're not yet sure about getting involved, just reread a few of these stories. You could contribute to a similar story that is still waiting to be created.

—Michael Piraino
Chief Executive Officer
National CASA Association

Resources

State CASA and GAL Organizations

The National CASA organization represents over 970 local community child advocate programs. Most of these programs are called CASA; others have names such as Guardian ad Litem (GAL), Child Advocates, or Voices for Children. Although the program names might vary from state to state, all share the same mission: to help abused and neglected children find safe homes and hope for the future. If you would like more information about the local community program near you, please contact the state CASA or GAL program listed below, or visit the National CASA website at www.nationalcasa.org.

Alabama CASA Network, Inc.
2806 Ruffner Road, Suite 111
Irondale, AL 35210-3927
205/833-1135

Alaska CASA
Office of Public Advocacy
900 W. 5th Avenue, Suite 525
Anchorage, AK 99501
907/269-3500

Arizona CASA Program/Arizona Supreme Court
Administrative Office of the Courts
1501 W. Washington Street, Suite 119A
Phoenix, AZ 85007-3231
602/542-9583

Arkansas State CASA Association
Administrative Office of the Courts
625 Marshall Street, Box 2100
Little Rock, AR 72201-1061
501/682-9403

California CASA Association
660 13th Street, Suite 300
Oakland, CA 94612
800/214-2272

Colorado CASA
1234 Bannock Street
Denver, CO 80204
303/623-5380

Children in Placement/CASA

300 Whalley Avenue
New Haven, CT 06511
203/784-0344

Court Appointed Special Advocates of DC

1522 K Street, NW, Suite 200
Washington, DC 20005-4961
202/289-8808

CASA Program/Family Court of Delaware

The New Castle County Courthouse
500 King Street, Suite 3500
Wilmington, DE 19801-3757
302/255-0071

Florida GAL Association

P.O. Box 973
Glen St. Mary, FL 32040
904/259-3476

Georgia CASA

1776 Peachtree Road, NW
Suite 219, South Tower
Atlanta, GA 30309-2307
404/874-2888

Volunteer Guardian ad Litem Program

Judiciary, State of Hawaii
P.O. Box 3498
Honolulu, HI 96811-3498
808/538-5930

Idaho CASA Association

152 East Main
P.O. Box 395
Jerome, ID 83338
208/320-3152

Illinois CASA

2 Lincoln Square
Urbana, IL 61801-3338
217/384-0284

Indiana Office of GAL/CASA

115 W. Washington, Suite 1080
Indianapolis, IN 46204-3714
317/232-2542

Iowa CASA Program

4th Floor, Lucas Building (DIA)
321 E. 12th Street
Des Moines, IA 50319-0083
515/242-6392

Kansas CASA Association

103 E. 27th Street, Unit C
Hays, KS 67601
785/625-3049

Kentucky CASA, Inc.

1110 College Street
Bowling Green, KY 42101
270/783-8458

Louisiana CASA Association
265 Third Street
Baton Rouge, LA 70801
985/370-8458

Maine CASA Program
West Bath District Court
147 New Meadows Road
West Bath, ME 04530-9704
207/442-0226

Maryland CASA Association
207 E. Redwood Street, Suite 204
Baltimore, MD 21202
410/244-1066

Massachusetts Court Appointed Special Advocates, Inc.
75 Palmer Street, No. 104
Quincy, MA 02169
617/471-3281

Michigan CASA Association
Children's Charter of the Courts of Michigan, Inc.
324 N. Pine Street, #1
Lansing, MI 48933-1024
517/482-7533

Minnesota Association of Guardians ad Litem, Inc.
P.O. Box 17358
Minneapolis, MN 55417-0358
612/728-5930

CASA Mississippi, Inc.
P.O. Box 6658
Diamondhead, MS 39525
601/352-5275

Missouri CASA Association
3200 Westcreek Circle
Columbia, MO 65203
573/441-0162

CASA/GAL of Montana
301 S. Park Avenue, Rm. 328
P.O. Box 203005
Helena, MT 59620-3005
406/841-2969

Nebraska CASA Association
315 S. 9th Street, #213
Lincoln, NE 68508
402/477-2788

8th Judicial District Court
CASA Family Division
601 N. Pecos Road, Room 460
Las Vegas, Nevada 89101
702/455-4306

CASA of New Hampshire, Inc.
P.O. Box 1327
44 Walnut Street
Manchester, NH 03105-1327
603/626-4600

CASA of New Jersey

667 Shunpike Road, Suite 4
Green Village, NJ 07935
973/410-9409

New Mexico CASA Network

4100 Menaul Boulevard, NE, Suite 2F
Albuquerque, NM 87110-2961
505/875-0978

CASA: Advocates for Children of New York State

99 Pine Street Suite C102
Albany, NY 12207
518/426-5354

North Carolina State GAL Program

100 E. Six Forks Road
P.O. Box 2448
Raleigh, NC 27602
919/571-4820

North Dakota Guardian ad Litem Project

University of North Dakota School of Law
Gillette Hall, Room 2
P.O. Box 7090
Grand Forks, ND 58202-7090
701/777-4913

Ohio CASA/GAL Association

261B E. Livingston Avenue
Columbus, OH 43215
614/224-2272

Oklahoma CASA Association

P.O. Box 54946
Oklahoma City, OK 73154
800/742-2272

Oregon Commission on Children & Families

CASA State Coordination Office
530 Center Street, NE, Suite 405
Salem, OR 97301
503/373-1283

Pennsylvania CASA Association

114 Walnut Street, Second Floor
Harrisburg, PA 17101
717/233-3118

Office of Court Appointed Special Advocate

Rhode Island Family Court
Room 211/One Dorrance Plaza
Providence, RI 02903-3922
401/458-3330

**South Carolina Office of the Governor—
Guardian ad Litem Program**

1205 Pendleton Street, Suite 440A
Columbia, SC 29201-3731
803/734-0663

South Dakota CASA Association

105 S. Euclid, Suite A
Pierre, SD 57501
605/945-0100

Tennessee CASA Association

501 Union Street, Suite 300-E
Nashville, TN 37219
615/242-8884

Texas CASA

1145 W. 5th Street, Suite 300
Austin, TX 78703
512/473-2627

Utah CASA

Administrative Office of the Courts
450 South State Street, Second Floor, Suite W22
P.O. Box 140403
Salt Lake City, UT 84114-0403
801/578-3957

Vermont GAL Program

Vermont Supreme Court
109 State Street
Montpelier, VT 05601
802/828-6551

CASA of the Virgin Islands

Legal Services of the Virgin Islands, Inc.
3017 Orange Grove
Christiansted Street, St. Croix, VI 00820-4375
340/773-2626

Department of Criminal Justice Services

805 E. Broad Street, 10th Floor
Richmond, VA 23219
804/786-6428

Washington State Association of CASA/GAL Programs

603 Stewart Street, Suite 206
Seattle, WA 98101-1229
206/667-9716

West Virginia CASA Network

P.O. Box 7553
Charleston, WV 25356-0553
304/776-5882

Wisconsin CASA Association

P.O. Box 301
Portage, WI 53901
608/742-5344

Sheridan County CASA Program

245 Broadway
P.O. Box 6022
Sheridan, WY 82801
307/672-0311 ext. 211 or 212

Special Thanks

Acknowledgments

Compiling and editing the foster youth essays contained in this book required the support and effort of many agencies, community organizations, and individuals. We are indebted to all who worked in collaboration with the National CASA Association to bring these touching and powerful essays and poems to you.

We would like to first thank the American Legion Child Welfare Foundation and the Office of Juvenile Justice and Delinquency Prevention for providing the funding that made production of this book possible.

Thanks also to the volunteers and staff of the nationwide network of state and local community CASA and GAL programs for making foster youth aware of the opportunity to submit their writing to National CASA.

We acknowledge Steve Bryant and his creative team at Publicis Dialog, Seattle, for helping to refine the concept behind this book and for finding a major talent like Antwone Fisher to write the book's foreword.

Our thanks to Keith Hefner with Youth Communications, Susan Weiss of Casey Family Programs, and Eve Malakoff-Klein of the Child Welfare League of America for working with their respective agencies to garner many of the youth essays contained in this book.

We are grateful to Kristen Kreisher Fletcher for editing the essays and creating the accompanying adult prologues. These prologues helped frame each youth's story, providing a greater understanding of the writer's circumstances and character. The design skills of Jennifer R. Geanakos provided a moving setting for the essays.

Our thanks to our Technical Editor, Janet Ward, CASA Regional Program Specialist, whose diligent and sensitive editing of each youth's essay helped to ensure that the youths' stories are well told and consistent with National CASA's standards for confidentiality.

Finally, this book would not exist without the youth who created the essays and poems printed here. By opening up their world to us through their writing, they are giving us the opportunity to better understand the lives of the more than half a million children and youth currently in the foster care system. It is a great gift, and we sincerely appreciate it.